# EPIC FINANCE JOURNEY

Navigating The future with advanced finance

Gold Harbor

Copyright© 2024 by GOLD HARBOR

All rights reserved. No part of this publication may be reproduced, distributed, or transmitted in any form or by any means, including photocopying, recording, or other electronic or mechanical methods, without the prior written permission of the publisher, except in the case of brief quotations embodied in critical reviews and certain other noncommercial uses permitted by copyright law.

Title: Epic Finance Journey

Author: Gold Harbor

Publication Year: 2024

For permission requests, contact the publisher at
ikhlafi1014@gmail.com

# TABLE OF CONTENTS

**TABLE OF CONTENTS**    **2**
**INTRODUCTION**    **13**
**Chapter 1: Understanding Advanced Financial Concepts**    **16**

    Hook: "In a world of rapid financial evolution, knowledge is your greatest asset."    16

Subchapter 1: Risk Management    16
- Utilizing advanced risk-management strategies to protect investments    16
- Diversification strategies across asset classes    17
- Implementing derivatives and hedge funds to reduce risk:    18

Sub-Chapter 2: Quantitative Analysis    19
- Using data-driven methods for investment decisions    19
- Application of statistical algorithms and models    20
- Understanding market trends through quantitative analysis    21

Subchapter 3: Behavioral Finance    22
- Identifying psychological biases in financial decision-making    22
- Strategies for overcoming emotional investment pitfalls    23
- Leveraging behavioral insights for better financial outcomes    24

Subchapter 4: Financial Engineering    25
- Designing complex financial instruments to fulfill specific needs    25
- Application of structured products in portfolio management:    26
- Engineering approaches for capital optimization and risk transfer    27

Sub-chapter 5: Macro-financial trends    28
- Analyzing the effects of global economic indicators on markets    28
- Positioning investments in response to geopolitical events    29
- Anticipating macroeconomic changes for strategic asset allocation    30

**Chapter 2: Advanced Investment Strategy    32**

Hook: "Unlock the power of sophisticated investment approaches."    32

Sub-Chapter 1: Alternative Investment    32
- Exploring venture capital and private equity opportunities    32
- Investing in infrastructure projects and real estate funds    33
- Investing in cryptocurrency and commodities to increase diversification    34

Sub-chapter 2: Comparison of Active and Passive Management    35
- Evaluating the advantages of active portfolio management    35
- Implementing passive investment strategies through ETFs and index funds    36
- Blending active and passive approaches

for optimal returns    37
Sub-chapter 3: High-frequency trading    38
- Understanding the mechanisms of high-frequency trading    39
- Assessing the risks and benefits of algorithmic trading    39
- Leveraging technology for rapid execution and arbitrage opportunities    40

Sub-chapter 4: Global Investment    41
- Navigating the worldwide markets and regulatory environments    42
- In global investment portfolios, hedging currency risk    42
- Identifying emerging markets for growth    43

Sub-chapter 5: Impact Investing    44
- Investing based on governance, social, and environmental (ESG) standards    45
- Evaluating social and financial outcomes on impact investments    46
- Incorporating sustainability into investment decisions    47

**Chapter 3: Advanced Portfolio Management Techniques**    **48**

Hook: "Master the art of optimizing your investment portfolio."    48

Sub-Chapter 1: Portfolio Optimization.    48
- Implementing Modern Portfolio Theory for Asset Allocation    48
- Balancing risk and return using efficient frontier analysis    49
- Utilizing methods of mean-variance optimization    50

Sub-Chapter 2: Factor-Based Investment    51
- Building portfolios based on variables including value, momentum, and size    51
- Understanding the academic research behind factor investing    52
- Implementing factor-based solutions to enhance returns    53

Sub-chapter 3: Dynamic Allocation of Assets    54
- Adapting portfolio allocations based on market conditions    54
- Incorporating strategies for tactical asset allocation    55
- Utilizing the use of dynamic risk management techniques    56

Subchapter 4: Portfolio Rebalancing    57
- Maintaining target asset allocations through periodic rebalancing    58
- Tax-effective rebalancing techniques    58
- Rebalancing based on market values and investment outlook    59

Sub-chapter 5: Risk Parity    60
- Allocating risk across asset classes rather than capital    61
- Implementing risk parity techniques for balanced portfolios    61
- Understanding Risk Parity's Benefits and Challenges    62

**Chapter 4: Advanced Financial Modeling    64**
Hook: "Harness the power of financial modeling to drive informed decisions."64

Sub-Chapter 1: Valuation Techniques    64
- Applying discounted cash flow (DCF)

analysis to a company's valuation   64
- Utilizing relative valuation methods such as P/E and P/B ratios   65
- Assessing the strengths and limitations of different valuation approaches   66

Sub-chapter 2: Scenario Analysis   67
- Evaluating potential outcomes in different scenarios   68
- Stress testing portfolios against adverse market conditions   68
- Incorporating scenario analysis into investment decision-making   69

Sub-chapter 3: Monte Carlo Simulation   70
- Simulating future asset price changes with Monte Carlo methods   71
- Assessing the probability of various investment outcomes   71
- Incorporating Monte Carlo simulation in procedures for risk management   72

Sub-Chapter 4: Models of Option Pricing   73
- Understanding the principles behind option pricing models   74
- The Black-Scholes model and its modifications are used to value options   74
- Applying option pricing models to derivatives trading and risk management   75

Sub-chapter 5: Financial Forecasting   76
- Using time series analysis to predict future financial performance   77
- Regression analysis for revenue and expense forecasting   78

Incorporating qualitative aspects into

financial forecasts ... 78

**Chapter 5: Advanced Risk Management Strategy** ... 80

    Hook: "Shield your wealth against uncertainties with advanced risk management." ... 80

  Sub-Chapter 1: Tail Risk Hedging ... 80
- Protecting portfolios against extreme market events ... 80
- Utilizing volatility derivatives and put options as tail-risk hedging strategies ... 81
- Managing downside risk without preserving upside potential ... 82

  Sub-Chapter 2: Value at Risk ... 83
- Using VaR to measure and manage portfolio risk ... 83
- Considering VaR's limitations as a risk measure ... 84
- Using Scenario Analysis and Stress Testing to Improve Risk Management ... 84

  Sub-chapter 3: Risk Management of Credit ... 85
- Identifying and managing credit risk in fixed-income portfolios ... 86
- Utilizing credit derivatives for risk transfer ... 87
- Monitoring credit spreads and credit rating changes ... 87

  Subchapter 4: Counterparty Risk ... 88
- In derivative transactions, managing counterparty risk ... 89
- Assessing counterparties' creditworthiness ... 89

- Putting netting and collateral agreements into action — 90

Sub-chapter 5: Operational Risk — 91
- Operational risk identification and management in financial institutions — 91
- Implementing risk-reduction methods and internal controls — 92
- To improve risk management techniques, learn from past operational failures — 93

**Chapter 6: Advanced Tax Planning Strategy — 95**

Hook: "Minimize your tax burden and maximize your after-tax returns." — 95

Sub-Chapter 1: Tax-efficient Investing — 95
- Organizing investments to minimize tax liabilities — 95
- Utilizing tax-advantaged accounts, such as 401(k)s and IRAs — 96
- Implementing tax-loss harvesting strategies — 97

Sub-Chapter 2: Business Tax Optimization — 98
- Choosing the right business structure for tax efficiency — 98
- Leveraging tax deductions and credits for business expenses — 99
- Implementing strategies for deferring or reducing corporation taxes — 99

Subchapter 3: International Tax Planning. — 100
- Managing the tax implications of cross-border transactions — 101
- Utilizing Tax Treaties and Transfer Pricing Strategies — 101
- Organizing international operations to

minimize taxation　　　　　　　　　　102
Subchapter 4: Estate Planning　　　　103
- Minimizing estate taxes through strategic planning　　　　　　　　　　　　　103
- Making use of trusts and other estate planning instruments　　　　　　　　104
- Ensure a smooth transfer of wealth to future generations　　　　　　　　　105

Subchapter 5: Tax Compliance and Reporting　　　　　　　　　　　　　106
- Maintaining compliance with tax legislation and regulations　　　　　　　106
- Establishing robust tax documentation and reporting protocols　　　　　107
- Navigating tax audits and resolving tax disputes　　　　　　　　　　　　107

## Chapter 7: Advanced Wealth Management Strategy　　　　　　　　　　　　109

Hook: "Build and preserve your wealth with sophisticated wealth management techniques."　　　　　　　　　　109

Sub-Chapter 1: Family Office Services　109
- Creating a family office for complete wealth management　　　　　　　　109
- Modifying investment plans to meet the needs of wealthy families　　　　　110
- Providing skilled financial assistance and concierge services　　　　　　　111

Subchapter 2: Philanthropic Planning　112
- Incorporating charitable giving into wealth management plans　　　　　112
- Maximizing the impact of charity

    initiatives   113
- Using tax-efficient methods to donate to charities   113

Sub-chapter 3: Legacy Planning   115
- Preserving family legacies through strategic planning   115
- Implementing strategies to transfer wealth to heirs and beneficiaries   116
- Addressing the issues of intergenerational wealth transfer   116

Subchapter 4: Lifestyle Planning   117
- Balancing wealth accumulation and lifestyle goals   118
- Creating personalized financial plans to achieve lifestyle objectives   118
- Managing expenses and cash flow to maintain the desired standard of living   119

Sub-Chapter 5: Concierge Wealth Management   120
- Obtaining Special Services and Investment Opportunities   121
- Applying individual wealth management solutions   121
- Providing holistic financial planning and advice services   122

## Chapter 8: Embracing the Future of Finance   124

    Hook: "Prepare for the next frontier in finance with cutting-edge insights."   124

Sub-Chapter 1: Fintech Innovation   124
- Using disruptive technologies in finance   124
- Exploring opportunities in machine

learning, AI, and blockchain 125
- Transforming traditional financial services with technology solutions 126

Sub-chapter 2: Decentralized Finance 127
- Understanding the Principles of Decentralized Finance 127
- Exploring DeFi applications, such as lending platforms and decentralized exchanges 128
- Assessing the opportunities and risks of investing in DeFi 129

Sub-Chapter 3: Sustainable Finance 130
- Integrating social and environmental factors in investment decisions 130
- Supporting environmentally conscious businesses and projects 131
- Financing climate resilience and renewable energy initiatives 132

Subchapter 4: The Globalization of Finance 133
- Managing the Changing Global Financial Landscape 133
- Adapting to regulatory and geopolitical shifts 134
- Taking advantage of opportunities in global trade and emerging markets 135

Subchapter 5: Financial Wellness 136
- Promoting wellness and financial literacy initiatives 136
- Empowering individuals to make informed financial decisions 137
- Creating a secure financial future through empowerment and education 138

**CONCLUSION** 139

# INTRODUCTION

In a world where financial markets pulse with the beat of global economies, understanding and navigating sophisticated finance is equivalent to carrying a powerful compass through unknown territory. Consider this: as of this year, worldwide financial assets totaled $900 trillion, a figure that is steadily increasing. However, within this immense sea of cash come both opportunity and risk, and the uneducated might quickly find themselves adrift in a tempest of uncertainty.

Imagine you're on a ship surrounded by dense fog, unsure which way leads to a safe harbor and which leads to perilous shoals. This metaphor captures the present financial landscape, where our decisions ripple through economies, affecting people well beyond our sphere. In such circumstances, ignorance is more than just a lack of knowledge; it is a liability. This is where our book, "Epic Finance Journey: Navigating the Future with Advanced Finance." comes in handy. Its goal is to be more than simply another book on finance but also a lighthouse for individuals looking to comprehend, harness, and prosper in the dynamic world of advanced finance. This book is an invaluable reference for prospective investors, seasoned professionals, and everyone wondering about the forces influencing our world.

We take you on a trip to demystify the complex workings of finance through its pages, giving you the knowledge and understanding you need to make wise decisions in a world growing more interconnected by the day. Every chapter acts as a torch, illuminating the route to financial literacy and expertise, from breaking down the subtleties of derivatives to figuring out the complexities of algorithmic trading.

But empowerment is our ultimate goal, not just comprehension. We think you can move beyond being a passive spectator and take an active role in determining your financial future by having a clear understanding of the fundamental ideas that guide financial markets.

This book contains real-world examples, case studies, and practical activities that will help you comprehend and enhance your analytical skills. Whether you're dealing with the complexity of risk management, investigating the possibilities of developing markets, or understanding the ramifications of monetary policy, our goal is to provide you with the knowledge and confidence you need to face any financial problem.

In an age where volatility is the new normal and uncertainty reigns supreme, the ability to negotiate the complexity of finance is more than simply a valued talent; it is a requirement. So join us on this adventure as we seek mastery.

# Chapter 1: Understanding Advanced Financial Concepts

**Hook:** "In a world of rapid financial evolution, knowledge is your greatest asset."

## Subchapter 1: Risk Management

In the ever-changing world of finance, the ability to successfully manage risk is critical. Whether you're an experienced investor or a beginner in the world of finance, recognizing risk and its ramifications might mean the difference between success and failure.

Risk management is not about completely avoiding danger; rather, it is about effectively analyzing and minimizing risk to safeguard investments and optimize profits. This subchapter digs into financial professionals' risk-management tactics and techniques.

- **Utilizing advanced risk-management strategies to protect investments**

Diversification and asset allocation are common tactics in traditional risk management, but they become more sophisticated in advanced finance.

Advanced risk management tools, including value-at-risk (VaR) models, stress testing, and scenario analysis, provide a more in-depth understanding of potential exposures and vulnerabilities.

Using quantitative models and statistical techniques, investors can better assess and control risks, allowing for a more sophisticated approach to portfolio management. Furthermore, advanced risk management tactics allow investors to quickly respond to changing market conditions, reducing losses and maximizing opportunities.

- **Diversification strategies across asset classes**

The age-old adage "don't put all your eggs in one basket" is still relevant in sophisticated finance, possibly even more so. Diversification is a critical component of risk management, distributing assets across asset classes, industries, and geographical locations to reduce correlation and mitigate the impact of adverse events.

This sub-chapter delves into the concept of strategic asset allocation, in which investors build portfolios depending on their risk tolerance, investment objectives, and time horizon. Diversification across asset classes, from equities and fixed income to alternative investments like real estate and commodities, can boost risk-adjusted returns and protect against market volatility.

- **Implementing derivatives and hedge funds to reduce risk:**

Advanced investors should have both hedge funds and derivatives in their toolbox because they present special chances to reduce risk and improve portfolio efficiency. Hedge funds can offer uncorrelated returns and downside protection in erratic markets because of their capacity to use a variety of investment strategies and alternative assets.

Similarly, flexible risk management solutions are provided by derivatives like futures, swaps, and options, which let investors speculate on future market trends, hedge against unfavorable price movements, and increase portfolio returns through leverage and arbitrage.

Hedge funds and derivatives, meanwhile, can be useful instruments for managing risk, but they also come with a unique set of dangers and complications. Success in advanced finance requires knowing when and how to employ them, as well as incorporating them into a comprehensive risk management framework.

Advanced financial concepts are built around risk management, which allows investors to traverse market uncertainty with confidence and agility.

Investors may protect their investments and capitalize on opportunities in an ever-changing financial landscape by using advanced risk management strategies, diversifying across asset classes, and utilizing hedge funds and derivatives.

## Sub-Chapter 2: Quantitative Analysis

In today's fast-paced financial world, where milliseconds can make or break a trade, quantitative analysis has become increasingly important. This subchapter dives into data-driven techniques, statistical models, and algorithms, demonstrating how they influence investing decisions and provide insights into market patterns.

- **Using data-driven methods for investment decisions**

Investment decisions no longer rely entirely on gut instinct or qualitative assessments. In today's digital age, massive volumes of data are created every second, providing investors with a wealth of knowledge. Data comes from a variety of sources, including financial statements, economic indicators, social media sentiment, and satellite photography.

Quantitative analysts take advantage of this data deluge, using advanced approaches to extract actionable information and make sound financial decisions. They can use statistical methodologies, machine learning algorithms, and data visualization tools to spot patterns, uncover anomalies, and anticipate future market trends with previously inconceivable precision.

- **Application of statistical algorithms and models**

Statistical models and algorithms are fundamental to quantitative analysis because they provide the basis of data-driven decision-making. These tools help investors better understand market dynamics and make more accurate predictions. They can be used in regression analysis to quantify the relationship between variables, time series models to forecast future prices, or machine learning algorithms to find hidden patterns in data.

In addition, technological developments have made it possible to create complex trading methods like algorithmic and high-frequency trading. These strategies take advantage of short-lived market opportunities and profit from inefficiencies by executing trades at breakneck speed using mathematical models and computer algorithms.

- **Understanding market trends through quantitative analysis**

Comprehending market dynamics is crucial in a world where a multitude of factors, from macroeconomic trends to geopolitical events, interact to move markets. Investors can interpret these trends through the lens of quantitative analysis, which can reveal hidden connections and casualties that are unseen by the human eye.

Through thorough statistical research and hypothesis testing, investors can effectively validate their investing plans and adjust to evolving market conditions. Additionally, investors can remain ahead of the curve by using quantitative analysis to spot new trends and strategically position themselves to take advantage of opportunities in the market before they become popular.

The way investors approach financial markets has shifted substantially as a result of quantitative analysis, bringing in an era of algorithmic trading and data-driven decision-making. Investors may easily navigate the market's complexities by leveraging statistical models and algorithms, which can also help them uncover hidden insights and gain a competitive advantage in a world that is becoming increasingly digital and data-driven.

# Subchapter 3: Behavioral Finance

In the world of finance, where rationality and logic are frequently assumed to be guiding principles, the discipline of behavioral finance illuminates an indisputable truth: humans are not always rational beings. This sub-chapter delves into the fascinating junction of psychology and economics, shedding light on the psychological biases that influence financial decision-making and providing techniques for avoiding these emotional errors.

- **Identifying psychological biases in financial decision-making**

From overconfidence and loss aversion to herd behavior and anchoring, the human mind is full of cognitive biases that can obscure judgment and lead to illogical investing choices. Behavioral finance tries to comprehend these biases and their impact on financial markets, questioning the conventional view of Homo as a rational agent.

Recognizing these psychological biases allows investors to better understand their thought processes and prevent illogical conduct. Whether it's the proclivity to hold onto failing assets in the hopes of a return or the desire to join the herd in a speculative frenzy, awareness is the first step toward minimizing the negative impacts of cognitive bias.

- ## Strategies for overcoming emotional investment pitfalls

To avoid emotional investment traps, you must be self-aware, have self-control, and be prepared to question deeply ingrained thought habits. This section goes into the various strategies that investors might use to manage their emotions and come to more reasonable judgments.

One such strategy is mindfulness, which involves cultivating an objective awareness of one's thoughts and feelings. Investors can improve their emotional regulation and resilience in the face of market changes by incorporating mindfulness methods such as meditation and deep breathing.

Another strategy is to establish and adhere to specific financial goals as well as a well-defined investment plan. Investors should avoid making impulsive decisions based on temporary market swings by following a disciplined investment plan and setting reasonable expectations.

- ## Leveraging behavioral insights for better financial outcomes

Although behavioral biases may result in illogical actions, they can also offer astute investors the chance to profit from inefficiencies in the market. The use of behavioral insights by investors to obtain a competitive advantage in the market is examined in this subchapter.

Contrarian investors, for instance, might take advantage of the herd mentality by taking advantage of market overreactions and mispricings to purchase when others are selling and sell when others are buying. Similarly, value investors might find inexpensive assets that the market has missed by utilizing cognitive biases like representativeness and anchoring.

Furthermore, behavioral insights can be used by legislators and financial advisors to create interventions that promote investors' improved financial decision-making. Policymakers can support the promotion of financial stability and well-being by structuring information in a way that appeals to people's psychological biases and steers them toward more logical decisions.

Behavioral finance provides a sophisticated grasp of how psychology affects financial judgment. Investors can successfully traverse the complexities of the market with more confidence if they are aware of psychological biases, put tactics in place to avoid emotional mistakes and use behavioral insights to improve financial outcomes.

## Subchapter 4: Financial Engineering

Financial engineering is the cutting-edge junction of finance, mathematics, and technology, where novel solutions are developed to satisfy the changing needs of investors and institutions. This sub-chapter delves into the intriguing realm of financial engineering, namely the creation of complex financial instruments, the use of structured products in portfolio management, and engineering solutions for risk transfer and capital optimization.

- **Designing complex financial instruments to fulfill specific needs**

Financial engineering is the act of constructing and changing financial products to achieve specific objectives, such as increasing returns, reducing risk, or capitalizing on unique investment possibilities. These instruments usually include complicated mathematical models, structured securities, and derivative contracts.

Convertible bonds, for example, offer investors a flexible method to strike a balance between income and growth by allowing them to profit from both the fixed-income characteristics of bonds and the potential upside of stocks. Similarly, without the requirement to retain the underlying assets, synthetic collateralized debt obligations (CDOs) can be structured to match the risk-return profile of traditional CDOs.

- **Application of structured products in portfolio management:**

Structured products play an important role in modern portfolio management, providing investors with bespoke solutions to meet their investment goals while limiting risk. These products mix derivatives, debt instruments, and other financial instruments to produce personalized investment strategies that match investors' risk tolerance and return expectations.

For example, principal-protected notes give downside protection while letting investors participate in the performance of an underlying asset or index, making them an appealing option for risk-averse investors seeking exposure to turbulent markets. Similarly, constant proportion portfolio insurance (CPPI) dynamically adjusts the allocation of risky and risk-free assets based on predetermined parameters, allowing investors to capitalize on upside potential while mitigating downside risk.

- ## Engineering approaches for capital optimization and risk transfer

Financial engineering also encompasses capital optimization and risk transfer strategies, which enable businesses to manage their balance sheets more effectively and inexpensively. This includes tactics like securitization, which pools assets and converts them into marketable securities to diversify risk and free up capital.

Credit derivatives, such as credit default swaps (CDS), allow investors to speculate on credit events or hedge against default risk by transferring credit risk from one entity to another. Financial engineers also utilize sophisticated risk models and analytical tools to assess and manage complex risks such as tail risk and systemic risk. This assists institutions in maintaining financial stability and protecting against unexpected events.

Financial engineering is a dynamic discipline that combines technological prowess and mathematical rigor to create customized solutions for investors and institutions. Financial engineers play an important role in influencing the direction of finance and propelling global economic growth, whether they are developing complex financial instruments, using structured products in portfolio management, or developing risk mitigation and capital optimization strategies.

# Sub-chapter 5: Macro-financial trends

Macroeconomic trends have enormous effects on the interwoven web of global finance, shaping market mood, driving investment flows, and directing the destiny of economies all over the world. This sub-chapter discusses the crucial relevance of monitoring macro-financial trends, investigating how global economic indicators affect markets, positioning investments in reaction to geopolitical events, and forecasting macroeconomic shifts for strategic asset allocation purposes.

- **Analyzing the effects of global economic indicators on markets**

Numerous economic indicators are used to gauge the health and vitality of a nation's economy, ranging from GDP growth and inflation rates to unemployment rates and central bank policies. Investors trying to traverse the intricacies of the global economy must comprehend the relevance of these indicators and how they interact with financial markets.

A strong GDP growth rate, for example, would indicate a thriving economy with lots of prospects for investment, but rising inflation rates might force central banks to tighten monetary policy, which might depress market mood. Through an analysis of these variables and their effects on asset prices, interest rates, and currency rates, investors may better position their portfolios and make more informed decisions.

- **Positioning investments in response to geopolitical events**

Trade tensions, political upheavals, and geopolitical conflicts are examples of geopolitical events that can have a significant impact on the financial markets, leading to volatility and uncertainty. The topic of this subchapter is how investors might profit from investment opportunities and manage geopolitical risks in the face of unrest.

For instance, investors may seek solace from market volatility by gravitating toward safe-haven assets like gold and government bonds during times of elevated geopolitical tensions. On the other hand, purchasing opportunities may arise as a result of geopolitical events in industries or geographical areas that are seen to be inexpensive or immune to geopolitical concerns.

- **Anticipating macroeconomic changes for strategic asset allocation**

Macro-financial trends give crucial strategic asset allocation insights, assisting investors in identifying new opportunities and dangers across asset classes and geographic regions. Investors can improve portfolio diversity and risk-adjusted returns by predicting macroeconomic changes and modifying their asset allocation accordingly.

For example, in preparation for an economic slowdown, investors may shift a larger share of their portfolio to defensive sectors like healthcare and consumer staples, which are less subject to economic cycles. During periods of economic prosperity, investors may shift their portfolios to cyclical sectors such as technology and industrials, which are expected to profit from strong economic development.

Macro-financial trends provide investors with insights into economic dynamics, geopolitical dangers, and investment opportunities. They act as a compass for those navigating the enormous world of global finance. Through the examination of worldwide economic indicators, the placement of investments in reaction to geopolitical developments, and the anticipation of macroeconomic changes for strategic asset allocation, investors can adeptly and confidently negotiate the intricacies of the global economy, thereby unleashing the possibility of enduring financial prosperity.

# Chapter 2: Advanced Investment Strategy

**Hook:** "Unlock the power of sophisticated investment approaches."

## Sub-Chapter 1: Alternative Investment

In an environment marked by low-interest rates, market volatility, and greater correlation across traditional asset classes, alternative investments have emerged as an appealing option for investors looking to diversify their portfolios and increase returns. This sub-chapter digs into alternative investment alternatives, including private equity and venture capital, real estate funds and infrastructure projects, and diversification with commodities and cryptocurrencies.

- **Exploring venture capital and private equity opportunities**

Venture capital and private equity provide investors with access to a diverse range of investment opportunities, including established organizations in the process of expanding or reorganizing and early-stage startups. These investments expose investors to assets that are not commonly found in open markets, with the potential for high returns and portfolio diversification.

Private equity investors generally buy ownership stakes in privately held businesses intending to increase their value over time through strategic initiatives, operational improvements, or financial restructuring. Venture capital, on the other hand, focuses on investing in firms with strong growth potential, typically in fields such as fintech, biotech, and artificial intelligence.

- ## Investing in infrastructure projects and real estate funds

Real estate and infrastructure investments allow investors to diversify their portfolios beyond traditional asset classes, generate consistent income streams, and hedge against inflation. Real estate funds pool investor funds to acquire and manage a diversified portfolio of properties, including residential, commercial, and industrial assets.

Infrastructure investments include a wide range of projects such as transportation, electricity, telecommunications, and utilities. These investments appeal to investors looking for long-term, steady returns because they frequently provide critical services to society and have little association with traditional asset classes.

- **Investing in cryptocurrency and commodities to increase diversification**

Cryptocurrencies and commodities are examples of alternative asset classes that have the potential for uncorrelated returns and special benefits related to diversification. Commodities are vital components of the world economy and can act as a hedge against inflation and exchange risk. Examples of commodities include gold, oil, and agricultural items.

As digital assets with the potential to upend established financial systems and expose investors to decentralized technology, cryptocurrencies like Bitcoin and Ethereum have grown in popularity. In a well-rounded investing portfolio, cryptocurrencies can provide diversification benefits and act as a buffer against the devaluation of fiat currencies, despite their high volatility and speculative nature.

Alternative investments provide a wide range of chances for investors to increase returns, control risk, and expand the diversification of their holdings outside of conventional asset classes. In an ever-changing financial landscape, advanced investment strategies can open up new doors for growth and prosperity, whether it's investing in real estate funds and infrastructure projects, looking into private equity and venture capital opportunities, or diversifying your portfolio with commodities and cryptocurrencies.

## Sub-chapter 2: Comparison of Active and Passive Management

There has long been debate in the realm of investment management about the benefits of active versus passive planning. This sub-chapter examines the advantages of active portfolio management as well as the possible benefits of combining active and passive approaches to maximize returns. Passive investment strategies are implemented using index funds and exchange-traded funds (ETFs).

- **Evaluating the advantages of active portfolio management**

To outperform the market, active portfolio management requires actively selecting investments and making strategic decisions. Active management advocates argue that competent portfolio managers may identify cheap stocks, capitalize on market inefficiencies, and generate alpha by selecting the appropriate stocks and timing the market.

Furthermore, active managers have the flexibility to adjust their portfolios in response to changing market conditions, economic trends, and geopolitical changes, which can decrease negative risk and increase returns. Nonetheless, data show that a large proportion of active managers fall short of their benchmarks over time, and active management incurs higher fees and transaction costs.

- **Implementing passive investment strategies through ETFs and index funds**

Passive investment methods aim to duplicate the performance of a market index or asset class by owning a diverse portfolio of securities in proportion to their weight in the index. ETFs and index funds are popular tools for executing passive strategies because they provide low-cost, transparent, and tax-efficient access to a diverse variety of asset classes and market segments.

Passive investors can earn market returns with little effort and cost by tracking large market indices like the S&P 500 or the MSCI World Index. Furthermore, passive strategies have low turnover, which decreases transaction costs and capital gains distributions, providing higher net returns for investors in the long run.

- **Blending active and passive approaches for optimal returns**

While the argument over active and passive management frequently pits one technique against the other, many investors understand the potential benefits of combining the two strategies to capitalize on their respective advantages. This hybrid technique, also known as smart beta or factor investing, aims to combine the advantages of active stock picking with the cost-effectiveness of passive indexing.

For example, factor-based ETFs may overweight equities with qualities such as low volatility, value, or momentum, which have historically outperformed the broader market. Combining these factor tilts with a passive core portfolio may allow investors to improve returns and manage risk more effectively than either technique alone.

The choice between active and passive management is ultimately determined by investors' tastes, risk tolerance, and investment goals. While active management has the potential to outperform, it comes with greater costs and unpredictability, whereas passive strategies provide low-cost exposure to broad market returns but may lag during periods of market inefficiencies. By carefully examining the merits of both techniques and prudently combining them, investors may create portfolios that strive to maximize returns while efficiently managing risk in an ever-changing financial landscape.

# Sub-chapter 3: High-frequency trading

A subtype of algorithmic trading known as high-frequency trading (HFT) is distinguished by extremely quick execution times, quick turnover, and the application of cutting-edge technology. This section delves into the workings of high-frequency trading, evaluates the advantages and disadvantages of algorithmic trading, and looks at ways that investors can use technology to take advantage of arbitrage opportunities and quick execution.

- **Understanding the mechanisms of high-frequency trading**

High-frequency trading uses sophisticated algorithms and cutting-edge equipment to conduct several deals in fractions of a second. These algorithms evaluate market data, recognize trends, and execute trades using predetermined rules and parameters.

HFT strategies use a variety of techniques, including market making, statistical arbitrage, and latency arbitrage. Market makers add liquidity to the market by simultaneously placing buy and sell orders and earning on the bid-ask spread. Statistical arbitrage techniques look for transient pricing inefficiencies across similar assets, whereas latency arbitrage strategies take advantage of differences in execution times across multiple trading venues.

- **Assessing the risks and benefits of algorithmic trading**

Algorithmic trading has various advantages, such as better liquidity, lower transaction costs, and improved market efficiency. By automating the trading process and removing human emotion, algorithms can execute deals with greater precision and regularity, reducing the impact of market noise and sentiment-driven volatility.

However, algorithmic trading carries risks, especially in the world of high-frequency trading. The speed and number of transactions can exacerbate market volatility, leading to flash crashes and systemic risk. Furthermore, the reliance on complicated algorithms and technology makes HFT firms exposed to technological flaws, software problems, and cyberattacks, which can have disastrous effects for financial markets.

- ## Leveraging technology for rapid execution and arbitrage opportunities

High-frequency trading relies heavily on technology, which allows corporations to execute deals with unprecedented speed and efficiency. Advanced trading platforms, low-latency networks, and co-location services enable HFT businesses to shorten execution times to microseconds, giving them a competitive advantage in today's fast-paced markets. Furthermore, HFT firms use technology to discover arbitrage opportunities and capitalize on temporary price differences across trading venues and asset classes. HFT businesses can profit from market inefficiencies by using sophisticated algorithms and real-time market data feeds to execute rapid-fire trading methods.

High-frequency trading, which uses technology and algorithms to execute deals with blazing-fast speed and accuracy, is a fundamental shift in the way financial markets function. HFT has advantages like lower transaction costs and more liquidity, but it also has drawbacks, including systemic fragility and market volatility. Through comprehension of the principles of high-frequency trading, evaluation of the advantages and disadvantages of algorithmic trading, and utilization of technology to facilitate swift execution and arbitrage prospects, investors can proficiently and perceptively maneuver through the intricacies of the contemporary digital financial terrain.

## Sub-chapter 4: Global Investment

Access to new markets, portfolio diversification, and capitalizing on emerging trends and economies are just a few of the benefits of global investing. This sub-chapter provides detailed information on managing global investment portfolios, navigating international markets and regulatory frameworks, and identifying growth opportunities in emerging markets.

- **Navigating the worldwide markets and regulatory environments**

Investing in overseas markets brings distinct obstacles and opportunities, such as variations in regulatory frameworks, accounting standards, and market structures. Before engaging in global investing, investors should become acquainted with the legal and regulatory requirements of each country, as well as the political and economic dangers associated with overseas markets.

Furthermore, cultural and language obstacles might make it difficult for investors to traverse international marketplaces. Building good ties with local partners, completing extensive due diligence, and being up-to-date on geopolitical changes are critical for success in global investing.

Investing abroad has many advantages despite these difficulties, such as diversification, access to economies with greater growth rates, and exposure to cutting-edge businesses and sectors that might not be well represented in home markets.

- **In global investment portfolios, hedging currency risk**

Currency risk, sometimes referred to as exchange rate risk, results from changes in foreign exchange rates and has the potential to affect the returns of international investment portfolios. Investors can use a variety of hedging techniques, such as futures contracts, options, and currency exchange-traded funds (ETFs), to reduce their exposure to currency risk.

Investors can protect themselves against unfavorable currency swings by locking in a future exchange rate for a predetermined amount of money using forward contracts. Options give flexibility and downside protection by giving investors the option, but not the duty, to buy or sell currencies at a predetermined price.

Investors can easily get exposure to foreign currencies without the hassles of dealing in the foreign exchange market directly by using currency exchange-traded funds (ETFs), such as those that follow the performance of currency baskets or actively managed currency strategies.

- **Identifying emerging markets for growth**

Emerging markets offer an appealing possibility for investors seeking growth and diversification. These economies, which are characterized by strong economic growth, expanding middle classes, and rising consumer demand, provide significant investment opportunities in a variety of sectors and industries.

However, investing in emerging markets carries greater risks, such as political unrest, currency volatility, and governance concerns. To find good possibilities in emerging markets, investors must perform extensive research, evaluate country-specific aspects such as economic fundamentals, demographic trends, and regulatory environments, and diversify their portfolios across different developing markets to reduce risk.

Additionally, investors can consider investing in emerging market-focused funds or exchange-traded funds (ETFs), which offer expert management and risk reduction as well as diversified exposure to a wide range of emerging market assets.

Global investment allows investors to broaden their market reach, diversify their portfolios, and profit from emerging markets and trends. Investors may unleash the potential for long-term success and wealth in an increasingly linked world by managing global investment portfolios effectively, hedging currency risk, and identifying growth opportunities in emerging economies.

# Sub-chapter 5: Impact Investing

A new paradigm in the financial industry, impact investing aims to provide investors with both financial returns and favorable social and environmental effects. This section explores the fundamentals of impact investing, including how to incorporate sustainability considerations into investment strategies, assess the financial and social returns on impact investments, and integrate environmental, social, and governance (ESG) criteria into investment decisions.

- ## Investing based on governance, social, and environmental (ESG) standards

In addition to financial returns, impact investing involves allocating capital to produce quantifiable positive social or environmental impact. Including environmental, social, and governance (ESG) considerations in investment decision-making is a key component of impact investing. These considerations include things like corporate governance, diversity and inclusion, labor standards, and carbon footprints.

Investors can find firms and initiatives that connect with their beliefs and contribute to beneficial social and environmental outcomes by including ESG criteria in their investment analysis. Furthermore, the inclusion of ESG principles can aid in risk mitigation, improve long-term performance, and promote responsibility and openness among invested companies.

- ## Evaluating social and financial outcomes on impact investments

Measuring the impact of investments poses particular problems because social and environmental outcomes are sometimes qualitative and difficult to measure. Nonetheless, impact investors use a variety of criteria and frameworks to evaluate and monitor the social and environmental performance of their portfolios, including the United Nations Sustainable Development Goals (SDGs) and the Global Impact Investing Network (GIIN) standards.

Impact investors assess the social and environmental effects of their investments in addition to their economic impact, intending to achieve competitive risk-adjusted returns. Research indicates that impact investing can yield competitive financial returns in the long run, together with beneficial social impact, even though short-term returns may be lower than typical investments.

- **Incorporating sustainability into investment decisions**

Sustainability factors are increasingly being included in investment decisions as investors acknowledge the necessity of solving global issues including climate change, inequality, and resource depletion. Sustainable investing includes a wide range of approaches, such as ESG integration, thematic investing, and shareholder involvement.

Investors can incorporate sustainability considerations into their investment strategies by focusing their portfolios on themes like renewable energy, sustainable agriculture, and affordable housing. Furthermore, investors can work with firms and legislators to promote positive change and encourage corporate responsibility and accountability.

Impact investing is a potent instrument that may be used to generate financial rewards while promoting positive social and environmental change. A more sustainable and just future for future generations can be built by investors through the integration of ESG criteria into investment decisions, the assessment of the impact of investments' social and financial returns, and the incorporation of sustainability considerations into investment strategies.

# Chapter 3: Advanced Portfolio Management Techniques

**Hook:** "Master the art of optimizing your investment portfolio."

## Sub-Chapter 1: Portfolio Optimization.

Effective portfolio management is at the heart of successful investment, and the art of managing risk and return can mean the difference. This sub-chapter delves into advanced portfolio optimization strategies, such as applying modern portfolio theory to asset allocation, balancing risk and return with efficient frontier analysis, and using mean-variance optimization techniques to produce optimal investment results.

- **Implementing Modern Portfolio Theory for Asset Allocation**

Harry Markowitz established modern portfolio theory (MPT), which introduced the concept of diversification and the trade-off between risk and return. According to MPT, investors can create portfolios that maximize expected return for a given level of risk or minimize risk for a given level of return by distributing capital among a diverse group of assets.

Investors can attain a more efficient frontier—where the risk of the portfolio is minimized for a given level of return, or the return is maximized for a given level of risk—by adding assets with low or negative correlations. By providing a framework for asset allocation that takes into account the covariance structure and projected returns of assets, MPT enables investors to manage their portfolios according to their investment goals and risk tolerance.

- **Balancing risk and return using efficient frontier analysis**

Efficient frontier analysis uses modern portfolio theory ideas to determine the optimal portfolio allocation that maximizes returns or reduces risk for a given level of return. The efficient frontier is the set of all potential portfolios that provide the highest expected return for a given level of risk or the lowest risk for the same level of return.

Efficient frontier analysis allows investors to visualize the risk-reward trade-off and determine the best portfolio allocation to maximize risk-adjusted return. By showing the expected return and volatility of multiple portfolios on a graph, investors can discover the efficient frontier and choose the portfolio that best aligns.

- **Utilizing methods of mean-variance optimization**

A quantitative method called mean-variance optimization (MVO) is used to create ideal portfolios that minimize risk and maximize expected return. In MVO, the weights of various assets in the portfolio are determined by solving a mathematical optimization problem to accomplish the intended risk-return trade-off.

Through the estimation of asset variances, covariances, and anticipated returns, investors can create an efficient frontier and choose the portfolio that provides the best-expected return at a given risk level or the lowest risk at a given return level. Taking into consideration their investment limits and preferred level of risk, MVO enables investors to methodically evaluate and optimize their portfolios using objective standards.

A key element of sophisticated portfolio management strategies is portfolio optimization, which enables investors to build portfolios that optimize returns while lowering risk. Investors can attain optimal investment outcomes and confidently and expertly navigate the intricacies of financial markets by employing mean-variance optimization techniques, implementing modern portfolio theory for asset allocation, and efficiently balancing risk and return through frontier analysis.

# Sub-Chapter 2: Factor-Based Investment

Factor-based investing is a systematic method of portfolio construction that takes advantage of specific aspects or qualities thought to influence performance in financial markets. This sub-chapter delves into the fundamentals of factor-based investing, such as building portfolios based on characteristics like value, momentum, and size, comprehending the academic research underpinning factor investing, and executing factor-based techniques for higher returns.

- **Building portfolios based on variables including value, momentum, and size**

Factor-based investing entails creating portfolios that favor specific features or qualities associated with greater returns. Some of the most commonly examined factors are:

1- Value stocks have low price-to-earnings (P/E) or price-to-book (P/B) ratios, indicating that they are undervalued in comparison to their fundamentals.
2- Momentum: Stocks with good prior performance tend to do strongly in the short term.
3- Size: Small-cap stocks have generally outperformed large-cap stocks in the long run.

By tilting portfolios toward these factors, investors hope to capture the related excess returns while preserving diversity and risk management.

## • Understanding the academic research behind factor investing

Factor investing is based on decades of academic study that has revealed persistent patterns in stock returns that cannot be explained by standard market risk (beta). Eugene Fama and Kenneth French's key study, known as the Fama-French Three-Factor Model, revealed that factors like value and size account for a considerable amount of the volatility in stock returns.

Subsequent research has revealed additional elements that contribute to explaining returns, including momentum, quality, and low volatility. The academic literature gives useful insights into factor return drivers, assisting investors in understanding the rationale for factor-based strategies and their potential for alpha generation.

- **Implementing factor-based solutions to enhance returns**

Factor-based strategies can be executed using a variety of methods, including factor tilts, smart beta ETFs, and quantitative investment strategies. Investors can build factor portfolios by overweighting equities or assets with favorable factor qualities and underweighting those that don't.

Smart beta ETFs, which track indices designed to capture specific variables, provide a simple and inexpensive approach for investors to obtain exposure to factor-based strategies. These ETFs use rules-based approaches to create portfolios that are weighted toward factors like value, momentum, or low volatility, giving investors diversified exposure to factor premia.

Factor models and multifactor portfolios are two types of quantitative investment techniques that use complex algorithms and statistical methods to identify and capitalize on factor-based anomalies in financial markets. These strategies seek to generate alpha by taking advantage of mispricings and inefficiencies associated with specific aspects.

Factor-based investing offers investors a methodical strategy to maximize gains by skewing portfolios in favor of specific factors or attributes associated with superior outcomes. Investors can potentially achieve superior risk-adjusted returns and navigate complex financial markets more efficiently by constructing portfolios based on value, momentum, and size, understanding the academic research behind factor investing, and implementing factor-based strategies for increased returns.

# Sub-chapter 3: Dynamic Allocation of Assets

A flexible method of managing a portfolio, dynamic asset allocation modifies allocations over time in reaction to shifting risk variables, market conditions, and economic trends. The fundamentals of dynamic asset allocation are covered in this sub-chapter, along with how to use dynamic risk management strategies, tactical asset allocation strategies, and portfolio adjustments based on market conditions.

- **Adapting portfolio allocations based on market conditions**

Continually assessing market circumstances and modifying portfolio allocations to take advantage of opportunities and control risks are key components of dynamic asset allocation. Market conditions can affect asset prices and correlations, requiring changes to portfolio allocations.

Examples of these conditions include changes in interest rates, inflation expectations, and geopolitical events. Investors may, for instance, allocate a larger portion of their portfolios to riskier assets during economic expansions, such as stocks and commodities, which typically perform better in bull market conditions. On the other hand, investors may allocate more to defensive assets like bonds and cash during times of market turbulence or economic depression to protect capital and reduce downside risk.

- **Incorporating strategies for tactical asset allocation**

An important aspect of tactical asset allocation (TAA) is the active change of portfolio allocations in response to investment opportunities and short-term market forecasts. In contrast to strategic asset allocation, which is based on long-term risk and return expectations, TAA seeks to capitalize on short-term inefficiencies and mispricings in financial markets.

Tactical asset allocation strategies may include market timing, in which allocations are adjusted in response to signals from technical or fundamental analysis, or sector rotation, in which investments are directed toward sectors or industries expected to outperform. To identify and grasp tactical opportunities, TAA requires a swift and scientific approach to asset allocation, as well as extensive study and analysis.

- **Utilizing the use of dynamic risk management techniques**

Techniques for dynamic risk management, which are intended to reduce portfolio risk and protect capital during times of market stress, are also included in dynamic asset allocation. These methods could include dynamic allocation to defensive assets based on predetermined risk thresholds or dynamic hedging strategies, in which investors utilize futures or options to guard against downside risk.

In addition, dynamic risk management strategies might include modifying portfolio exposures in reaction to shifting market volatility or trends by using volatility targeting, trend-following, or stop-loss orders. Investors can improve risk-adjusted returns and guard against significant drawdowns in unfavorable market situations by actively managing portfolio risk.

A proactive approach to portfolio management is represented by dynamic asset allocation, in which allocations are changed in reaction to shifting risk factors and market conditions. Investors can navigate the complexity of financial markets with agility and resilience by adjusting portfolio allocations based on market conditions, incorporating tactical asset allocation strategies, and using dynamic risk management techniques. This can potentially improve long-term investment outcomes and preserve capital in difficult environments.

# Subchapter 4: Portfolio Rebalancing

Portfolio rebalancing is an important part of effective portfolio management since it ensures that investments remain consistent with investors' goals, risk tolerance, and market conditions. This subchapter delves into portfolio rebalancing principles, such as maintaining target asset allocations through periodic rebalancing, tax-efficient rebalancing strategies, and rebalancing based on market valuations and the investment outlook.

- **Maintaining target asset allocations through periodic rebalancing**

Periodic rebalancing is the process of realigning portfolio allocations to their target weights at regular periods, which are commonly quarterly, semiannually, or annual. Rebalancing keeps portfolios diversified and aligned with investors' risk preferences, preventing departures from the desired asset allocation over time.

For example, imagine an investor's desired asset allocation of 60% equities and 40% bonds. If equities outperform bonds over a certain period, the portfolio's equity allocation may rise above 70%. Rebalancing entails selling some stocks and buying bonds to restore the portfolio's original 60/40 allocation.

- **Tax-effective rebalancing techniques**

In taxable investment accounts in particular, tax-efficient rebalancing strategies seek to reduce the tax implications of portfolio rebalancing. Within tax-advantaged accounts, like IRAs or 401(k)s, where dividends and capital gains are tax-deferred, one popular strategy is to give rebalancing top priority.

To balance capital gains and lower taxable income, tax-loss harvesting also entails selling investments that have witnessed losses. Investors can reduce the effect of taxes on their portfolio rebalancing by systematically harvesting losses and matching gains.

- **Rebalancing based on market values and investment outlook**

  In addition to routine rebalancing, investors have the option to rebalance their portfolios based on these factors. Investors may adjust their allocations, for instance, if particular asset classes exhibit unfavorable risk-return characteristics or rise above historical averages.

  For example, during periods of market fervor or outrageous prices, investors may reduce their exposure to pricey assets and raise their allocations to defensive or discounted assets. Conversely, during periods of market crises or undervaluation, investors may opportunistically increase their exposure to attractively priced assets with strong long-term prospects.

  Additionally, investors may decide to rebalance their portfolios in response to shifts in macroeconomic trends, geopolitical events, or changes in their outlook for their investments. Throughout an investing horizon, investors can reduce risks and seize opportunities by being proactive and alert in monitoring market circumstances and making necessary adjustments to their portfolios.

Portfolio rebalancing is an essential component of efficient portfolio management since it keeps investments in line with investors' risk tolerance and goals. Through the implementation of tax-efficient rebalancing strategies, periodic rebalancing to maintain target asset allocations, and rebalancing under market valuations and investment outlooks, investors can effectively manage their portfolios for sustained success and skillfully traverse the intricacies of financial markets.

## Sub-chapter 5: Risk Parity

Instead of allocating capital, risk parity is a portfolio construction method that distributes risk across asset classes to generate balanced portfolios that can withstand a range of market and economic situations. The concepts of risk parity are examined in this sub-chapter, along with how to allocate risk among asset classes, use risk parity techniques to create balanced portfolios and comprehend the advantages and drawbacks of risk parity.

- **Allocating risk across asset classes rather than capital**

Traditional portfolio creation approaches typically allocate capital among asset classes based on their predicted returns and correlations. Risk parity, on the other hand, uses a different approach, allocating risk equally among asset classes, independent of predicted returns or past volatility.

Risk parity strives to develop portfolios that are diversified and balanced, with each asset contributing equally to the overall risk of the portfolio. This strategy ensures that no single asset class dominates the portfolio's risk profile, lowering the possibility of significant drawdowns during market downturns.

- **Implementing risk parity techniques for balanced portfolios**

Numerous methods, such as risk-based weighting, optimization algorithms, and leveraging, can be used to achieve risk parity strategies. Equal risk contribution (ERC) is a popular strategy in which assets are weighted so that each asset adds the same amount of risk to the portfolio as a whole.

An alternative strategy is risk parity, which aims to target a particular level of portfolio volatility and involves dynamically adjusting the weights of the portfolio to sustain a consistent level of risk over time. To boost the portfolio's exposure to riskier assets, including stocks or commodities, while keeping a balanced risk profile, leveraged risk parity techniques entail borrowing money.

- **Understanding Risk Parity's Benefits and Challenges**

Improved risk-adjusted returns, lower portfolio volatility, and increased diversification are just a few of the many benefits that risk parity may provide. Risk parity portfolios, which distribute risk evenly across asset classes, are more resistant to market and economic shocks and less dependent on the performance of any single asset class.

However, risk parity has some limitations, including the need for exact risk assessment and projection as well as the danger of leverage-induced losses during times of market stress. Furthermore, risk parity approaches may perform badly under some market conditions, such as rising interest rates or rapid changes in market correlations.

Risk parity is a method of building balanced portfolios that can withstand a range of market and economic conditions. It does this by spreading risk throughout asset classes as opposed to capital. Through the application of risk parity techniques for balanced portfolios and a comprehension of the advantages and difficulties associated with risk parity, investors can build portfolios that aim to maximize risk-adjusted returns and prudently and confidently negotiate the intricacies of financial markets.

# Chapter 4: Advanced Financial Modeling

**Hook:** "Harness the power of financial modeling to drive informed decisions."

## Sub-Chapter 1: Valuation Techniques

At the core of financial decision-making is valuation, which offers perceptions of the inherent value of investments, businesses, and assets. This sub-chapter examines advanced valuation strategies, such as using relative valuation techniques like P/E and P/B ratios, applying discounted cash flow (DCF) analysis for firm valuation, and evaluating the benefits and drawbacks of various valuation methodologies.

- **Applying discounted cash flow (DCF) analysis to a company's valuation**

A basic technique for valuing companies is discounted cash flow (DCF) analysis, which calculates the present value of future cash flows while accounting for the time value of money. The process of doing a DCF analysis involves projecting the company's future cash flows, discounting them to their present value using a suitable discount rate—such as the WACC or the company's cost of capital—and determining the intrinsic value of the business.

Using the rigorous and detailed framework provided by DCF analysis for company valuation, investors can assess a company's underlying value based on its ability to create cash flow. DCF analysis provides a foundation for well-informed investment decisions by discounting future cash flows to their present value while accounting for the risk and uncertainty associated with the business's operations.

- ## Utilizing relative valuation methods such as P/E and P/B ratios

Relative valuation techniques provide information about a company's valuation multiples, such as the price-to-earnings (P/E) and price-to-book (P/B), by comparing the company's valuation to those of its competitors or industry standards.For simple and rapid value comparisons between businesses and industries, relative valuation techniques are extensively employed.

The price that investors are ready to pay for each dollar that the company generates in earnings is measured by the P/E ratio, which is computed by dividing the stock price of the company by its earnings per share (EPS). In a similar vein, the P/B ratio assesses how well a firm is valued concerning its net assets by contrasting its market capitalization with its book value of equity.

- ## Assessing the strengths and limitations of different valuation approaches

Every valuation strategy has advantages and disadvantages, so investors should carefully weigh which approach is best for their particular situation and investment scenario. A company's intrinsic value can be viewed comprehensively and prospectively through DCF analysis, although it does need precise future cash flow forecasts and the choice of suitable discount rates.

Conversely, relative valuation techniques offer rapid and easy comparisons of valuation multiples between businesses, but they could ignore variations in growth prospects, risk profiles, and qualitative aspects. Relative valuation techniques can also result in mispricing or overvaluation since they are susceptible to shifts in investor expectations and market sentiment.

Advanced financial modeling tools are essential for directing investment strategies and generating educated decisions. Investors can obtain valuable insights into the intrinsic value of assets and make informed investment decisions by employing relative valuation techniques like P/E and P/B ratios, applying discounted cash flow (DCF) analysis for company valuation, and evaluating the advantages and disadvantages of various valuation approaches.

# Sub-chapter 2: Scenario Analysis

In financial modeling, scenario analysis is an effective technique for evaluating possible outcomes under various sets of assumptions and market conditions. The principles of scenario analysis are examined in this sub-chapter, along with how to use scenario analysis to inform investment decisions, stress test portfolios against volatile markets, and assess possible outcomes under various scenarios.

- **Evaluating potential outcomes in different scenarios**

In scenario analysis, a variety of realistic scenarios that represent different market, economic, and geopolitical conditions are constructed, and their possible effects on investment portfolios are evaluated. Investors can learn about a variety of possible outcomes and pinpoint the main factors influencing portfolio performance in various scenarios by simulating various scenarios.

Various degrees of economic growth, inflation, interest rates, and market volatility are represented by the optimistic, base case, and pessimistic scenarios, for instance. Investors can evaluate a portfolio's resistance to varying market situations and adjust their investing strategy by examining how the portfolio performs in each scenario.

- ## Stress testing portfolios against adverse market conditions

Stress testing includes exposing portfolios to extreme or adverse market conditions to assess their resilience and vulnerability to shocks. Stress tests evaluate portfolio performance during times of market volatility, economic downturns, or unanticipated occurrences such as geopolitical crises or natural disasters.

Sharp falls in asset prices, spikes in volatility, unexpected changes in interest rates, and liquidity problems are all possible stress test situations. Stress testing portfolios against these situations allows investors to uncover potential flaws, concentration risks, and vulnerabilities in their portfolios and take proactive steps to reduce them.

- **Incorporating scenario analysis into investment decision-making**

Scenario analysis is important in investment decision-making because it provides investors with useful information about the potential risks and possibilities associated with various market scenarios. By incorporating scenario analysis into their investment process, investors can make more informed decisions and create solid investment strategies that can withstand changing market conditions.

Scenario analysis, for example, can assist investors in assessing the impact of macroeconomic trends, industry disruptions, regulatory changes, or geopolitical events on their portfolios, allowing them to adjust asset allocations, risk management strategies, and hedging approaches accordingly. By evaluating a variety of possibilities and their potential consequences, investors can better plan for uncertainty and adjust their portfolios to shifting market dynamics.

Stress testing portfolios against unfavorable scenarios, analyzing possible outcomes under various sets of assumptions and market conditions, and incorporating scenario analysis into financial decision-making are all made possible with the use of scenario analysis. Investors can make better decisions, manage risk more skillfully, and confidently and resiliently negotiate the intricacies of financial markets by modeling various scenarios, stress-testing portfolios, and implementing scenario analysis into their investment process.

# Sub-chapter 3: Monte Carlo Simulation

In financial modeling, Monte Carlo simulation is a potent statistical approach that is used to anticipate future changes in asset prices and evaluate the likelihood of different investment outcomes. The fundamentals of Monte Carlo simulation are examined in this sub-chapter. These include utilizing Monte Carlo methods to simulate future asset price movements, determining the likelihood of different investment outcomes, and integrating Monte Carlo simulation into risk management procedures.

- **Simulating future asset price changes with Monte Carlo methods**

Monte Carlo simulation generates a huge number of random scenarios based on the probability distributions of key variables, including asset returns, volatility, and correlations. Monte Carlo methods provide a comprehensive and probabilistic perspective of the probable range of investment outcomes by simulating hundreds, if not millions, of different future scenarios.

In the context of stock prices, Monte Carlo simulation may entail simulating future stock returns using historical return distributions, volatility estimates, and correlation matrices. By simulating a large number of future stock price routes, investors can analyze the possibility of various price trajectories and prospective investment returns.

- **Assessing the probability of various investment outcomes**

Monte Carlo simulation allows investors to calculate the likelihood of different investment outcomes under various scenarios and market conditions. By studying the distribution of simulated outcomes, investors can determine the range of probable returns, downside risks, and tail events for their investment portfolios.

Monte Carlo simulation, for example, can reveal the possibility of meeting specified investment objectives, such as target returns or wealth accumulation targets, as well as the likelihood of incurring portfolio drawdowns or losses that surpass defined thresholds. By calculating the likelihood of various outcomes, investors can make more informed decisions and create risk management strategies that are suited to their risk tolerance and investment goals.

- ## Incorporating Monte Carlo simulation in procedures for risk management

When adding uncertainty and variability to risk management procedures, Monte Carlo simulation is a useful tool. Investors can evaluate the effect of various risk factors on portfolio performance and pinpoint risk sources and potential weaknesses by simulating hundreds of possible future scenarios.

Monte Carlo simulation, for instance, can be used to stress test portfolios against unfavorable market circumstances, such as interest rate shocks, market downturns, or geopolitical crises. Investors can evaluate their portfolio's resistance and vulnerability to various risk variables and take proactive steps to manage risks by modeling the implications of these scenarios on portfolio returns and volatility.

Monte Carlo simulation is an effective tool for forecasting future asset price movements, assessing the chance of various investment outcomes, and incorporating uncertainty into risk management procedures. Investors can improve their decision-making skills, manage risk effectively, and confidently and resiliently navigate complex financial markets by modeling hundreds of probable future scenarios and studying the distribution of simulated outcomes.

# Sub-Chapter 4: Models of Option Pricing

The theoretical value of option contracts is ascertained through the application of basic financial modeling tools called option pricing models. The concepts behind option pricing models are examined in this sub-chapter, along with how to value options using the Black-Scholes model and its variations and use option pricing models in risk management and derivatives trading.

- **Understanding the principles behind option pricing models**

The foundation of option pricing models is the idea of arbitrage-free pricing, which holds that an option's price should account for both its inherent value and any risk premium related to the price uncertainty of the underlying asset. By taking into account variables including the price of the underlying asset, the amount of time before expiration, volatility, interest rates, and dividend yield, these models seek to define the fair value of options.

Stochastic calculus and probability theory, two topics in mathematical finance, serve as the foundation for the ideas underlying option pricing models. According to these models, asset prices move in a random walk or geometric Brownian motion, with drift and volatility components characterizing price fluctuations.

- ### The Black-Scholes model and its modifications are used to value options

Constructed in 1973 by Fischer Black and Myron Scholes, the Black-Scholes model is a popular model for pricing options. The European-style options that are limited to exercise at expiration are valued using the theoretical framework that this model offers.

Considerations included in the Black-Scholes model are the underlying asset's volatility, time to expiration, strike price, current stock price, and risk-free interest rate. The Black-Scholes model determines the theoretical or intrinsic value of an option, often known as its fair value, by solving a partial differential equation derived from stochastic calculus.

The Black-Scholes model has been extended and modified to handle many forms of options, including American-style options (which can be exercised at any time before expiration), dividend-paying options, and stochastic volatility options. These models, such as the binomial option pricing model and the Heston model, better reflect real-world option pricing dynamics.

- ## Applying option pricing models to derivatives trading and risk management

Option pricing models are critical in derivatives trading and risk management because they allow investors to determine the fair value of options, develop hedging strategies, and control risk exposure. By pricing options using mathematical models, traders can detect mispriced options and implement effective trading strategies based on their future market expectations.

Additionally, option pricing models are widely utilized in risk management, especially concerning structured products and option portfolios, to measure and control portfolio risk. Through the examination of option pricing's sensitivity to shifts in fundamental variables like volatility and asset prices, risk managers can evaluate the effects of various scenarios on portfolio performance and adjust risk mitigation tactics accordingly.

Option pricing models offer a framework for evaluating option contracts and determining their fair value, making them indispensable instruments in financial modeling. Investors and risk managers can make better judgments by comprehending the underlying theories of option pricing models, valuing options using models like the Black-Scholes model and its variations, and utilizing option pricing models in derivatives trading and risk management.

# Sub-chapter 5: Financial Forecasting

As it offers insights into future financial performance and directs strategic activities, financial forecasting is an essential component of financial planning and decision-making. The fundamentals of financial forecasting are covered in this subchapter. These include employing time series analysis to predict future financial performance, regression analysis to estimate revenue and expenses, and incorporating qualitative aspects into financial forecasts.

- **Using time series analysis to predict future financial performance**

To estimate future financial performance, time series analysis entails examining past data to find patterns, trends, and relationships over time. These patterns are then extrapolated into the future. Moving averages, exponential smoothing, and autoregressive integrated moving average (ARIMA) models are a few time series forecasting techniques.

Time series analysis, for instance, may be used in revenue forecasting to find long-term trends, cyclical swings, and seasonal patterns in sales income by examining historical sales data. Analysts can produce revenue estimates for the future by fitting time series models to previous data and accounting for variables like seasonality, market trends, and economic conditions.

- **Regression analysis for revenue and expense forecasting**

A statistical technique called regression analysis is used to forecast and determine the correlation between one or more independent variables, often known as predictors, and a dependent variable, the outcome. Regression analysis is a widely used technique in financial forecasting to estimate the relationship between revenue, expenses, and other relevant factors.

For example, in revenue forecasting, analysts might utilize regression analysis to identify the key drivers of revenue growth, such as advertising spending, macroeconomic data, and customer demographics.

Analysts can create regression models utilizing historical data to forecast future income based on changes in these crucial drivers.

## Incorporating qualitative aspects into financial forecasts

In addition to quantitative data, financial predictions frequently include qualitative elements such as industry trends, competitive dynamics, legislative changes, and management judgment. Qualitative aspects offer useful insights into the larger corporate environment and can be used in conjunction with quantitative analysis to estimate future financial success.

Qualitative components in revenue forecasting, including market research, customer surveys, industry publications, and management interviews, can provide insights into customer preferences, competitive positioning, and developing trends. By including qualitative aspects in financial projections, analysts can improve forecast accuracy and robustness while also capturing the complete range of factors influencing future financial performance.

Financial forecasting, which provides insights into future financial performance and guides strategic initiatives, is a critical tool for financial planning and decision-making. Analysts can make better decisions, predict future trends, and confidently and strategically adjust their plans to changing market conditions by employing time series analysis to forecast future financial performance, regression analysis for revenue and expense forecasting, and qualitative factors in financial forecasts.

# Chapter 5: Advanced Risk Management Strategy

**Hook:** "Shield your wealth against uncertainties with advanced risk management."

## Sub-Chapter 1: Tail Risk Hedging

In the turbulent world of financial markets, protecting portfolios from extreme occurrences is critical. This sub-chapter discusses tail-risk hedging, which tries to protect portfolios from major downturns while retaining exposure to possible gains. We look at the basics of tail risk hedging, tactics like put options and volatility derivatives, and the delicate balance between reducing downside risk and keeping upside potential.

- **Protecting portfolios against extreme market events**

Tail risk hedging is intended to reduce the impact of uncommon but catastrophic market downturns, sometimes known as "tail events" or "black swan events." These low-probability but high-impact events might result in large losses for unprepared investors.

Tail risk hedging aims to decrease the possible impact of extreme events on portfolio performance rather than eliminate all downside risk. Protecting against tail risks allows investors to strengthen their portfolios and reduce the danger of catastrophic losses.

- **Utilizing volatility derivatives and put options as tail-risk hedging strategies**

Put options are one of the most common tail-risk hedging strategies. Put options allow the holder the right, but not the responsibility, to sell an asset at a predetermined price (the strike price) within a specified timeframe (until expiration).

Investors can reduce their exposure to downside risk and efficiently hedge against asset value declines by purchasing put options on individual stocks or broad market indices. Furthermore, volatility derivatives, such as VIX futures or options, can be used to hedge against market volatility spikes, which typically occur during times of market stress.

- **Managing downside risk without preserving upside potential**

One of the most difficult aspects of tail-risk hedging is balancing downward risk management with upside potential preservation. While hedging methods can protect against extreme losses, they also have costs, such as option premiums or the drag on returns caused by owning defensive assets.

To manage this trade-off, investors may use dynamic hedging techniques, which modify hedging amounts in response to market conditions and risk assessments. By regularly monitoring market dynamics and changing hedging positions as needed, investors can tailor their hedging strategy to the current risk environment while still partaking in possible market gains.

Advanced risk management techniques must include tail risk hedging since it protects investors from extreme market events while maintaining upside potential. Investors can reduce the impact of tail risks on their portfolios and deal more confidently and resiliently with the uncertainties of the financial markets by employing tactics like volatility derivatives and put options.

# Sub-Chapter 2: Value at Risk

Value at Risk (VaR) is a popular risk management statistic that quantifies the potential loss of portfolio value over a certain time horizon and confidence level. This sub-chapter delves into the fundamentals of value at risk (VaR), such as measuring and managing portfolio risk with VaR, evaluating the limitations of VaR as a risk measure, and improving risk management through stress testing and scenario analysis.

- **Using VaR to measure and manage portfolio risk**

Value at Risk (VaR) calculates the possible decrease in a portfolio's value at a specific confidence level (e.g., 95% or 99%) over a given time horizon, usually one day. VaR gives investors a way to quantify and control their exposure to possible losses by providing a single numerical metric that captures the downside risk of a portfolio.

A portfolio with a one-day 95% VaR of $1 million, for instance, has a 5% chance of losing more than $1 million during the following trading day. VaR can be computed by a variety of techniques, each having advantages and disadvantages, such as parametric estimation, Monte Carlo simulation, and historical simulation.

- **Considering VaR's limitations as a risk measure**

VaR is a useful tool for assessing portfolio risk, but investors should be aware of some of its limitations. One disadvantage of VaR is that it only provides a partial picture of the risk of catastrophic losses and may underestimate the frequency of tail-risk events, especially during periods of significant market volatility or stress. VaR also presupposes that asset returns are normally distributed, which may not be the case in real-world scenarios, particularly when dealing with assets with non-normal or fat-tailed returns.

Furthermore, VaR lacks information about the timing and magnitude of potential losses that may occur beyond its threshold, necessitating the adoption of additional risk measurements and analytic methods to supplement it.

- **Using Scenario Analysis and Stress Testing to Improve Risk Management**

Investors frequently combine VaR with scenario analysis and stress testing to overcome its shortcomings and enhance risk management techniques. Stress testing is the process of exposing portfolios to extreme or unfavorable market conditions to evaluate their shock resistance and durability.

On the other hand, scenario analysis entails creating a variety of believable situations and evaluating how they might affect the performance of a portfolio. Investors can obtain valuable insights into the possible risks and vulnerabilities of their portfolios and formulate effective risk mitigation strategies by integrating stress testing and scenario analysis into their risk management activities.

Value at Risk (VaR) is a useful risk management statistic that calculates the possible decline in a portfolio's value over a particular time horizon with a given degree of confidence. VaR is a helpful way to summarize portfolio risk, but investors should be mindful of its limits. Investors can improve their risk management procedures and more confidently and resiliently negotiate the vagaries of the financial markets by adding stress testing and scenario analysis to VaR.

## Sub-chapter 3: Risk Management of Credit

Credit risk management is critical in fixed-income portfolios since the risk of failure or credit degradation can have a significant impact on investment returns. This subchapter covers the fundamentals of credit risk management. These include tracking credit spreads and credit rating changes, employing credit derivatives to transfer credit risk, and analyzing and mitigating credit risk in fixed-income portfolios.

- **Identifying and managing credit risk in fixed-income portfolios**

Credit risk refers to the possibility of default or a fall in the creditworthiness of fixed-income issuers. Investors assess credit risk in fixed-income portfolios using a variety of criteria, including industry dynamics, macroeconomic trends, issuer credit quality, financial indicators such as leverage and interest coverage ratios, and industry dynamics.

Risk monitoring, credit research, and diversification are all required for credit risk reduction. Diversifying across issuers, industries, and credit quality can reduce the impact of defaults on portfolio performance and distribute credit risk. Furthermore, rigorous credit analysis allows investors to identify and avoid high-risk assets by assessing issuer fundamentals, industry trends, and credit ratings.

- **Utilizing credit derivatives for risk transfer**

Credit derivatives are financial products that enable investors to transfer or hedge credit risk exposure. Credit default swaps (CDS) and credit-linked notes (CLNs) are two common types of credit derivatives. CDSs protect against default by a single issuer or reference firm, while CLNs provide exposure to the credit risk of underlying assets.

Credit derivatives allow investors to hedge credit risk in fixed-income portfolios, improve credit risk management, and diversify portfolios. For example, investors can buy CDS contracts to protect against bond or portfolio defaults, or they can use CLNs to get credit risk exposure without actually holding the underlying bonds.

- **Monitoring credit spreads and credit rating changes**

Credit spreads, or the yield premium of corporate bonds over risk-free government bonds, are a key measure of credit risk in fixed-income markets. Widening credit spreads often signal worsening credit conditions and increasing credit risk, while narrowing spreads indicate better credit conditions and lower risk.

Furthermore, monitoring credit rating changes by rating agencies offers information on changes in issuer creditworthiness and probable credit risk events. Rating agency downgrades can cause price decreases in impacted bonds, increasing credit risk for holders of those assets.

In fixed-income portfolios, where the risk of failure or credit degradation can materially affect investment returns, credit risk management is crucial. Investors can improve their credit risk management techniques and more confidently and resiliently navigate the complex fixed-income markets by assessing and mitigating credit risk through diversification, credit analysis, and risk monitoring; using credit derivatives for credit risk transfer; keeping an eye on credit spreads and credit rating changes.

## Subchapter 4: Counterparty Risk

Counterparty risk is an important concern in derivative agreements because parties rely on one another to meet contractual obligations. This subchapter digs into the basics of controlling counterparty risk in derivative transactions, such as assessing counterparties' creditworthiness and putting in place collateral agreements and netting arrangements to reduce risk.

- **In derivative transactions, managing counterparty risk**

The risk of a counterparty's default on a derivative contract, which could result in financial losses for the other party, is referred to as counterparty credit risk or counterparty risk. To safeguard their interests and ensure the proper operation of financial markets, participants in the derivatives market must efficiently manage counterparty risk.

- **Assessing counterparties' creditworthiness**

One of the most critical tasks in managing counterparty risk is to assess counterparties' creditworthiness. Market actors judge counterparties using variables such as credit ratings, liquidity, and operational prowess. Credit ratings from rating agencies, while not the primary criteria, can be used to assess counterparty credit risk. Market participants conduct their credit analyses in addition to credit ratings.

This research entails reviewing financial documents, calculating leverage ratios, studying cash flows, and assessing counterparties' risk management methods.

Market participants can utilize this complete evaluation to make well-informed decisions about engaging in derivative transactions with specific counterparties.

- **Putting netting and collateral agreements into action**

Market participants regularly employ collateral agreements and netting arrangements to mitigate counterparty risk. Collateral agreements safeguard derivative exposures and limit potential losses in the event of counterparty default by requiring the posting of collateral, such as cash or securities. Collateralization reduces credit risk by providing a source of funding to cover losses and increasing the credibility of derivative transactions.

Netting arrangements enable counterparties to decrease total counterparty risk by offsetting and aggregating several derivative positions into a single net exposure. Netting arrangements make the settlement process easier and lower counterparty credit exposure, resulting in better capital allocation and risk management.

In derivative transactions, managing counterparty risk is critical to preserving market participants' interests and ensuring the financial system remains stable. Market participants can effectively mitigate counterparty risk and navigate derivative markets with greater confidence and resilience by assessing counterparties' creditworthiness, establishing collateral agreements, and establishing netting arrangements.

# Sub-chapter 5: Operational Risk

Financial institutions are highly concerned about operational risk, which includes the possibility of suffering losses as a result of insufficient or malfunctioning internal procedures, systems, personnel, or outside circumstances. The concepts of recognizing and managing operational risks in financial institutions, putting internal controls and risk mitigation measures in place, and strengthening risk management practices by learning from prior operational failures are all covered in this subchapter.

- **Operational risk identification and management in financial institutions**

Financial institutions are susceptible to operational risks from a variety of sources, such as mistakes, fraud, system malfunctions, violations of compliance, and outside incidents like cyberattacks or natural disasters. Maintaining the stability and safety of financial institutions as well as the interests of stakeholders requires identifying and managing these risks.

Risk identification entails evaluating the institution's business processes, technological systems, human resources, and external factors—all of which may be potential sources of operational risk. Implementing controls, processes, and procedures is the main goal of risk management techniques to mitigate identified risks and lessen the possibility and consequence of operational failures.

- **Implementing risk-reduction methods and internal controls**

Internal controls in financial organizations provide a framework for risk assessment, monitoring, and mitigation. They are thus a critical component of operational risk management. Internal controls, which include systems, processes, procedures, and policies, are used to maintain financial reporting integrity, protect assets, and comply with regulatory requirements.

Common internal controls and risk mitigation strategies include the separation of responsibilities, authorization and approval procedures, frequent audits and reviews, employee education and awareness campaigns, and technological controls such as intrusion detection systems, firewalls, and encryption. Strong internal controls can help financial institutions become more robust to risks and less prone to experiencing operational disruptions.

- **To improve risk management techniques, learn from past operational failures**

Processing errors, fraud incidents, and data breaches are all examples of operational failures that give financial institutions valuable lessons about how to enhance their risk management processes. Comprehensive post-mortem investigations can help firms identify the root causes of operational failures, system vulnerabilities, and opportunities to improve their risk management frameworks.

Some key lessons that can be learned from previous operational failures include strengthening supervision and governance structures, developing crisis management and incident response capabilities, increasing staff awareness and training, improving internal controls, and upgrading technology systems. Implementing a culture of resilience and continuous improvement can help financial firms reduce the likelihood of future operational breakdowns.

Financial institutions have a great deal of concern about operational risk, which calls for strong risk management procedures to properly detect, evaluate, and reduce risks. Financial institutions can increase their resistance to operational risks and keep stakeholders' trust by putting internal controls and risk mitigation measures in place, learning from previous operational mistakes, and consistently enhancing risk management procedures.

# Chapter 6: Advanced Tax Planning Strategy

**Hook:** "Minimize your tax burden and maximize your after-tax returns."

## Sub-Chapter 1: Tax-efficient Investing

Tax planning is an important part of wealth management, and using advanced tactics can dramatically minimize tax costs, boosting after-tax profits. This subchapter digs into tax-efficient investing, including how to arrange investments to reduce tax liabilities, how to use tax-advantaged accounts like IRAs and 401(k), and how to execute tax-loss harvesting techniques.

- **Organizing investments to minimize tax liabilities**

By carefully distributing assets across taxable and tax-advantaged accounts, investors can optimize their portfolios to reduce their tax obligations. The goal of tax-efficient investing is to prioritize tax-efficient tactics, such as buying tax-efficient funds or choosing long-term investments over short-term transactions, and to take into account the tax ramifications of various asset classes and investment vehicles.

To protect their profits from immediate taxes, investors can, for instance, transfer tax-inefficient assets—like actively managed mutual funds or high-yield bonds—to tax-advantaged accounts. To benefit from favorable tax treatment, tax-efficient assets, such as municipal bonds or index funds, might, on the other hand, be held in taxable accounts.

- **Utilizing tax-advantaged accounts, such as 401(k)s and IRAs**

Individual retirement funds (IRAs) and 401(k) retirement plans are two types of tax-advantaged funds that offer considerable tax breaks that can help with long-term wealth growth. Typically, pre-tax or tax-deductible contributions can be made to these accounts, and investment earnings grow tax-deferred until withdrawn in retirement.

Investors can reduce their current tax burden while investing for retirement by taking advantage of employer-sponsored retirement plans and tax-advantaged account contributions. In addition, Roth IRAs and Roth 401(k)s provide for tax-free withdrawals in retirement, offering tax diversity and flexibility in dealing with future tax demands.

- **Implementing tax-loss harvesting strategies**

Realizing capital losses on underperforming investments to offset capital gains and lower taxable income is known as tax-loss harvesting. Without materially changing their investment strategy, investors can benefit from tax advantages by selling investments that have unrealized losses and reinvesting the profits in comparable but distinct securities.

In taxable investment accounts, where capital gains taxes may apply to investment gains, tax-loss harvesting can be very beneficial. Investors can maximize their long-term after-tax profits and optimize their tax outcomes by methodically harvesting losses throughout the year.

A key element of sophisticated tax planning tactics is tax-efficient investment, which helps investors reduce their tax obligations and increase their after-tax returns. Investors can improve their long-term wealth accumulation objectives and optimize their tax results by employing tax-loss harvesting tactics, using tax-advantaged accounts like 401(k)s and IRAs, and structuring assets to minimize tax liabilities.

# Sub-Chapter 2: Business Tax Optimization

For companies to maximize revenues and keep their competitive edge in the market, tax optimization is essential. This subsection delves into business-specific tax optimization tactics, such as selecting the most advantageous business structure to minimize taxes, taking advantage of business expense tax deductions and credits, and putting corporate tax deferral or reduction plans into action.

- **Choosing the right business structure for tax efficiency**

The first step in helping businesses optimize their taxes is choosing the right business structure. The tax ramifications and benefits of various business arrangements, including partnerships, corporations (C- and S-corporations), limited liability companies (LLCs), and sole proprietorships, differ.

For instance, business income can "pass through" to owners' tax returns through pass-through companies like partnerships and S-Corporations. This can lower overall tax liability by preventing double taxation at the corporate and individual levels. C-Corporations, on the other hand, might benefit from reduced corporation tax rates or be qualified for certain tax breaks and credits.

- **Leveraging tax deductions and credits for business expenses**

Businesses can improve their tax positions by maximizing deductions and credits for qualified business costs. Salaries and wages, rent, utilities, supplies, marketing expenses, and asset depreciation are all examples of common deductible company expenses. Businesses may also be eligible for a variety of tax credits, including the R&D tax credit, energy efficiency tax credits, and small company healthcare tax credits.

Businesses can decrease their taxable income and overall tax liability by properly managing and documenting business expenses, as well as exploiting available deductions and credits. Implementing good spending management and accounting processes is critical for achieving tax savings while maintaining compliance with tax legislation.

- **Implementing strategies for deferring or reducing corporation taxes**

Businesses can use a variety of tactics to defer or minimize corporation taxes, including timing income and expenses, using tax deferral mechanisms, and capitalizing on tax planning possibilities. To improve their tax status, corporations may accelerate deductions or defer income recognition to future tax years.

Furthermore, businesses might look at tax planning options, such as cost segregation studies, to expedite depreciation deductions for specific assets and lower taxable income. Leveraging tax-deferred retirement plans for employees, as well as developing employee benefit programs, can help firms save money while attracting and retaining staff.

For companies to reduce their tax obligations and increase their profits, tax optimization is crucial. Businesses can improve their tax situations and financial performance in a cutthroat market by utilizing tax deductions and credits for company expenses, selecting the best business structure for tax efficiency, and putting plans in place to postpone or lower corporation taxes.

## Subchapter 3: International Tax Planning.

International tax planning is critical for firms doing cross-border transactions to negotiate the intricacies of foreign tax systems and optimize their tax position. This sub-chapter delves into international tax planning tactics, such as controlling the tax consequences of cross-border transactions, leveraging tax treaties and transfer pricing strategies, and structuring foreign businesses for tax efficiency.

- **Managing the tax implications of cross-border transactions**

Because different countries have different tax laws, rules, and jurisdictions, cross-border transactions present special tax issues. The tax ramifications of overseas transactions, such as income recognition, withholding taxes, and foreign tax credits, must be carefully considered by businesses.

Businesses that trade internationally, for instance, may run into tax problems with import/export taxes, value-added taxes (VAT), and customs duties. Multinational companies that have overseas subsidiaries also have to deal with the challenges of managing tax obligations in several jurisdictions and repatriating earnings.

- **Utilizing Tax Treaties and Transfer Pricing Strategies**

Tax treaties play an important role in international tax planning because they provide direction on how to allocate taxing rights across countries and prevent income from being taxed twice. Businesses can use tax treaties to reduce withholding taxes on cross-border payments like dividends, interest, and royalties while also optimizing their tax structures.

Transfer pricing is the pricing of commodities, services, and intangible assets moved between linked organizations within multinational corporations. Businesses can comply with transfer pricing requirements and disburse earnings tax-efficiently between jurisdictions by setting arm's length prices for intra-group transactions.

- **Organizing international operations to minimize taxation**

Companies can set up tax-efficient holding structures, legal entities, and jurisdictions to optimize tax efficiency in their global operations. Creating regional offices, holding corporations, or intellectual property (IP) holding firms in countries with advantageous tax regimes are examples of common techniques.

To reduce overall tax costs and consolidate ownership of international subsidiaries, organizations can, for instance, create holding companies in low-tax jurisdictions. Businesses can also optimize the tax advantages of licensing and royalty income by organizing their intellectual property ownership in jurisdictions with advantageous IP tax regimes.

Businesses involved in cross-border transactions must plan for international taxes to minimize tax risks and maximize their tax situations. Businesses can improve their financial performance and global competitiveness in an increasingly interconnected world by managing the tax consequences of cross-border transactions, leveraging tax treaties and transfer pricing tactics, and structuring foreign operations for tax efficiency.

## Subchapter 4: Estate Planning

In order to manage their assets, reduce their tax obligations, and guarantee a smooth transfer of wealth to future generations, individuals and families must engage in estate planning. This section looks at estate planning techniques, such as using trusts and other mechanisms to minimize estate taxes and make sure that money is passed onto future generations in an orderly manner.

- **Minimizing estate taxes through strategic planning**

Estate taxes are imposed on the transfer of assets from one generation to the next after an individual passes away. They are often referred to as inheritance taxes or death taxes.

Using a variety of tax-saving techniques and exemptions, strategic estate planning seeks to reduce estate taxes. A popular tactic to lower the amount of the taxable estate is to give away assets while still living. Individuals can transmit assets to heirs tax-free, subject to certain limitations, by utilizing the annual gift tax exclusion and lifetime gift tax exemption. A thorough estate plan that includes beneficiary designations, trusts, and wills can also reduce estate taxes by ensuring that assets are disbursed effectively and following the individual's desires.

- **Making use of trusts and other estate planning instruments**

Trusts are effective estate planning instruments that let people give assets to beneficiaries while keeping control over the distribution and management of those assets. Trusts have several advantages, such as chances for tax planning, asset protection, and the avoidance of probate.

To minimize inheritance taxes and provide beneficiaries with tax-free liquidity, irrevocable life insurance trusts (ILITs) can be utilized to remove life insurance proceeds from the taxable estate. In a similar vein, beneficiaries may receive income from charitable remainder trusts (CRTs) and charitable lead trusts (CLTs), which both lower estate taxes and promote good causes.

- **Ensure a smooth transfer of wealth to future generations**

Estate planning is more than just lowering taxes; it is also about ensuring a smooth transfer of wealth to future generations. This entails creating a complete estate plan that tackles critical issues such as guardianship of minor children, healthcare directives, and asset distribution preferences. Regular evaluation and modification of estate plans are required to account for changes in personal circumstances, tax regulations, and financial objectives. Individuals can build individualized estate plans that match their specific requirements and goals by consulting with skilled estate planning professionals such as attorneys, financial consultants, and tax specialists.

To manage their assets, reduce their tax obligations, and guarantee a smooth transfer of wealth to future generations, individuals and families must engage in estate planning. Through the smart use of trusts and other estate planning tools, avoiding estate taxes, and guaranteeing a seamless transfer of wealth to future generations, people can safeguard their legacies and make sure that their loved ones receive the care they desire.

# Subchapter 5: Tax Compliance and Reporting

Tax compliance and reporting are critical for people and corporations to meet their tax-related duties. This sub-chapter delves into tactics for adhering to tax rules and regulations, establishing effective tax reporting and documentation systems, handling tax audits, and settling tax disputes.

- **Maintaining compliance with tax legislation and regulations**

Individuals and corporations must comply with tax rules and regulations to avoid penalties, fines, and legal consequences. Compliance entails comprehending and complying with applicable tax rules, completing accurate and timely tax returns, and paying taxes in full and on time.

Individuals must record all sources of income, claim eligible deductions and credits, and meet tax responsibilities at the federal, state, and municipal levels. Tax compliance for businesses includes a variety of tasks, such as deducting and remitting payroll taxes, collecting and remitting sales taxes, and filing corporate income tax returns.

- **Establishing robust tax documentation and reporting protocols**

Robust tax reporting and documentation systems are necessary to ensure accurate reporting of income, credits, and deductions, as well as to support tax positions in the event of audits or disputes. To comply with legal requirements and support tax returns, individuals and organizations need to maintain comprehensive records of their income, expenses, assets, obligations, and transactions.

For individuals, this may entail submitting income, bank, and investment statements in addition to receipts for tax-deductible expenses. Businesses must maintain complete accounting records, financial statements, payroll records, and transactional paperwork to comply with tax laws.

- **Navigating tax audits and resolving tax disputes**

Although tax audits and disputes with tax authorities can be a difficult and time-consuming process, people and businesses can efficiently handle these challenges with the right preparation and representation. It is crucial to react quickly, provide the necessary paperwork and information, and assist tax authorities in the event of a tax audit or disagreement.

To handle tax audits and settle disputes with tax authorities, individuals and corporations can seek professional assistance from tax consultants, attorneys, or enrolled agents. If required, seasoned experts can offer advice on handling audit queries, settling disputes, contesting audit results, and defending clients in court or administrative procedures.

For people and companies to meet their tax duties and preserve their legal and financial integrity, tax compliance and reporting are crucial. Both individuals and corporations can reduce risks, prevent fines, and guarantee peace of mind in their tax affairs by adhering to tax rules and regulations, putting in place reliable tax reporting and documentation procedures, and getting professional help when necessary.

# Chapter 7: Advanced Wealth Management Strategy

**Hook:** "Build and preserve your wealth with sophisticated wealth management techniques."

## Sub-Chapter 1: Family Office Services

Family office services are the pinnacle of wealth management, offering affluent people and families comprehensive solutions tailored to their specific requirements. This sub-chapter delves into the creation of family offices, the tailoring of investment strategies for high-net-worth families, and the provision of concierge services and specialized financial guidance.

- **Creating a family office for complete wealth management**

A family office is an organization dedicated to monitoring the financial affairs of rich families. The primary purpose of a multi-family office (MFO) or a single-family office (SFO) is to transmit, grow, and protect money for subsequent generations. Establishing a family office requires customizing the office's governance, services, and operations to meet the family's goals, values, and preferences.

The family office coordinates a variety of financial services, including investment management, financial planning, tax optimization, estate planning, charitable giving, and lifestyle management. By combining all of these services under one roof, families get more control, accountability, and personalization over their wealth management strategy.

- **Modifying investment plans to meet the needs of wealthy families**

High-net-worth families require customized investing strategies due to their unique investment objectives, risk tolerances, and time horizons. Family offices work directly with their clients to develop investment strategies that align with their beliefs, preferences, and financial goals.

These approaches often incorporate a wide portfolio of assets, such as equities, bonds, real estate, hedge funds, private equity, and alternative investments. Family offices use complex investment methods such as asset allocation, manager selection, and risk management to enhance portfolio returns while minimizing risk and volatility.

- **Providing skilled financial assistance and concierge services**

In addition to investment management, family offices offer specialist financial advice and concierge services to wealthy families. Some of these services include lifestyle management, travel, education, insurance, charitable advising, and succession preparation.

Family offices serve as trusted consultants, providing personalized care, proactive guidance, and access to unique opportunities. They help clients navigate complex financial decisions, reduce tax liabilities, and achieve long-term objectives by combining a wide range of services and resources.

The ultimate in wealth management is provided by family office services, which give wealthy people and families all-inclusive solutions catered to their particular requirements. Family offices assist clients in building, preserving, and transferring wealth between generations while accomplishing their financial objectives and aspirations. They do this by establishing family offices, customizing investment strategies, and offering concierge services and expert financial guidance.

# Subchapter 2: Philanthropic Planning

Philanthropic planning is a key component of sophisticated wealth management, allowing individuals and families to make a significant contribution to society while optimizing tax methods and fulfilling personal beliefs. This sub-chapter investigates the incorporation of charity giving into wealth management plans, the design of philanthropic activities for the greatest benefit, and the use of tax-efficient philanthropic donation tactics.

- **Incorporating charitable giving into wealth management plans**

Philanthropic planning entails including charitable giving as a key component of wealth management strategies. It enables individuals and families to connect their financial resources with their personal ideals and make significant contributions to issues they care greatly about. Individuals and families can leave a lasting legacy of giving by incorporating philanthropy into their wealth management plans.

When incorporating charity giving into wealth management plans, individuals and families take into account their philanthropic goals, budgetary limits, tax implications, and desired impact. They may adopt a systematic strategy for giving, such as allocating a percentage of their income or assets to charitable causes, establishing a donor-advised fund, or forming a private foundation.

- **Maximizing the impact of charity initiatives**

Planning philanthropically effectively entails organizing charitable endeavors to have the greatest possible impact and to solve urgent societal issues. The philanthropic endeavors of individuals and families might be concentrated on causes or issues that hold personal significance to them, such as poverty reduction, healthcare, education, or environmental conservation.

Individuals and families can maximize the impact of their philanthropy by implementing strategic approaches like measuring results and outcomes, working with credible nonprofits or social enterprises, conducting in-depth research, and encouraging accountability and transparency in their philanthropic endeavors.

- **Using tax-efficient methods to donate to charities**

There are several tax advantages to charitable giving, and families and individuals can make the most of their philanthropic contributions by using tax-efficient planning techniques. For instance, contributions made to approved charities are typically tax-deductible, which lowers total tax obligations and taxable income.

Individuals and families might explore different approaches to maximize tax efficiency, like donating valuable assets, like stocks or real estate, rather than cash, to avoid paying capital gains taxes. To facilitate charitable giving while accomplishing particular tax planning goals, they may also make use of tax-advantaged structures like donor-advised funds, charitable remainder trusts, or charitable lead trusts.

A key component of sophisticated wealth management is philanthropic planning, which enables people and families to maximize tax benefits and uphold personal principles while also having a significant positive social impact. Individuals and families can leave a lasting legacy of giving that benefits communities and future generations by utilizing tax-efficient strategies for charitable donations, integrating charitable giving into wealth management plans, and organizing philanthropic initiatives for maximum impact.

# Sub-chapter 3: Legacy Planning

For wealthy people and families to maintain their riches, values, and legacies for future generations, legacy planning is essential. This sub-chapter explores the significance of safeguarding family legacies via intergenerational asset transfer issues, heir and beneficiary wealth transfer techniques, and strategic planning.

- **Preserving family legacies through strategic planning**

Legacy planning entails developing a comprehensive strategy to preserve and perpetuate affluent families' values, assets, and traditions over generations. It extends beyond financial prosperity to include non-financial factors such as family values, culture, and philanthropic efforts.

Strategic legacy planning entails establishing the family's mission, vision, and values, communicating shared goals and aspirations, and creating governance structures to assist decision-making and succession planning. Families can form family constitutions, advisory boards, or family councils to help with communication, consensus building, and the continuation of their family history.

- **Implementing strategies to transfer wealth to heirs and beneficiaries**

Wealth transfer is an essential component of legacy planning because it enables wealthy families to pass on their assets to future generations in a way that is both tax-efficient and egalitarian. Successful asset transfer plans include taking into account unique requirements and circumstances, matching financial goals with family values, and minimizing tax implications.

Commonwealth transfer strategies involve the drafting of wills, trusts, and other estate planning tools to transfer assets to heirs and beneficiaries in line with the family's wishes. Families can use generation-skipping transfer schemes, lifetime gifting, and charitable giving to move money while maximizing tax benefits and preserving family legacies.

- **Addressing the issues of intergenerational wealth transfer**

Rich families confront unique challenges in intergenerational wealth transmission, such as priority conflicts, communication failures, and inheritance disputes. To solve these challenges, legacy planning encourages unity and teamwork, open and honest communication, and heirs' preparedness for their roles and responsibilities.

Families can help prepare the next generation for money management, leadership, and decision-making by participating in proactive education and training efforts. They may also implement systems such as family retreats, mentorship programs, and family meetings to encourage communication, create trust, and strengthen family bonds.

To protect their fortune, principles, and legacies for future generations, wealthy people and families must engage in legacy planning. Families may make a lasting impact and guarantee the continuation of their legacies for future generations by carefully planning for legacy preservation, putting effective asset transfer plans into place, and resolving intergenerational wealth transfer difficulties.

## Subchapter 4: Lifestyle Planning

Advanced wealth management includes lifestyle planning, which focuses on matching financial resources with individual goals and desires. This section delves into the significance of striking a balance between accumulating wealth and achieving lifestyle goals, designing customized financial plans, and effectively handling spending and cash flow to sustain the intended way of life.

- **Balancing wealth accumulation and lifestyle goals**

Wealth growth is not an end in itself but rather a means to achieving one's preferred lifestyle and financial independence. Lifestyle planning entails finding a balance between building wealth for the future and enjoying the present. Individuals and families must establish their lifestyle goals, values, and priorities before making intelligent financial resource allocation decisions.

Individuals and families who understand their lifestyle goals can create specific targets for wealth growth, savings, and investing methods. They can prioritize spending on experiences, activities, and objects that provide fulfillment and happiness while guaranteeing long-term financial security and stability.

- **Creating personalized financial plans to achieve lifestyle objectives**

To achieve long-term financial well-being and match financial resources with lifestyle goals, personalized financial planning is crucial. It entails evaluating present financial situations, establishing reasonable objectives, and creating specialized plans to reach those objectives while taking into account lifestyle choices and ambitions.

Budgeting, savings objectives, investment strategies, risk management, retirement planning, and estate planning components are all possible components of financial plans. Individuals and families can maximize their financial resources, reduce risks, and confidently pursue their desired lifestyle by tailoring financial plans to their requirements and circumstances.

- **Managing expenses and cash flow to maintain the desired standard of living**

Achieving financial objectives and sustaining the desired lifestyle over time require efficient cash flow planning and cost control. Evaluating spending patterns, classifying expenses as discretionary or non-discretionary, and setting spending priorities under values and priorities for the lifestyle are all part of lifestyle planning.

To efficiently manage cash flow and prevent overspending, individuals and families can put tactics like budgeting, tracking expenses, avoiding debt, and automating savings into practice. Additionally, they might reassess and modify their spending habits regularly in reaction to evolving objectives, situations, and market dynamics.

A key component of sophisticated wealth management is lifestyle planning, which focuses on matching financial resources with individual aspirations and lifestyle objectives. Individuals and families can attain financial freedom and live the lifestyle they choose while guaranteeing long-term financial security and sustainability by striking a balance between wealth accumulation and lifestyle objectives, developing individualized financial plans, and efficiently managing expenses and cash flow.

## Sub-Chapter 5: Concierge Wealth Management

Concierge wealth management is a specialized approach to wealth management that provides rich people and families with exclusive investment possibilities and services, personalized wealth management solutions, and comprehensive financial planning and consulting services. This sub-chapter discusses the benefits of concierge wealth management and how it meets the specific needs of high-net-worth clients.

- **Obtaining Special Services and Investment Opportunities**

Concierge wealth management provides high-net-worth clients with special investing options that the general public may not have. Direct real estate investments, hedge funds, venture capital agreements, private equity investments, and other alternative investments are all possible options.

Using their extensive networks and industry connections, concierge wealth managers can identify unique investment opportunities with the potential for significant returns and portfolio diversification. To meet the complicated needs of a wealthy clientele, these opportunities usually include a higher level of customization, personalized attention, and due diligence.

- **Applying individual wealth management solutions**

High-net-worth individuals receive customized solutions from concierge wealth management, which are based on their particular financial goals, preferences, and circumstances. Working closely with their clients to fully understand their objectives, time horizon, risk tolerance, and liquidity needs, wealth managers create customized investment plans.

Tailored wealth management solutions may encompass activities such as asset allocation, risk management, lifestyle management, tax optimization, and charitable advising. Wealth managers work as trusted advisers, providing clients with ongoing support, strategic guidance, and proactive direction to help them achieve their goals and navigate challenging financial decisions.

- **Providing holistic financial planning and advice services**

Concierge wealth management extends beyond investment management to provide comprehensive financial planning and advising services that cover all facets of a client's financial life. Wealth managers adopt a complete approach to wealth management, taking into account aspects such as income, expenses, assets, obligations, taxes, insurance, estate planning, and legacy planning.

Concierge wealth managers assist customers in gaining better clarity, confidence, and control over their financial affairs by offering comprehensive financial planning and advising services. They act as a single point of contact for multiple financial services and resources, streamlining the wealth management process and allowing clients to focus on what is most important to them.

Rich people and families can receive specialized wealth management services, individualized investment opportunities, and comprehensive financial planning and consulting services through concierge wealth management. Concierge wealth managers assist high-net-worth individuals in achieving their financial objectives, protecting their wealth, and having peace of mind over their financial matters by utilizing their knowledge and resources.

# Chapter 8: Embracing the Future of Finance

**Hook:** "Prepare for the next frontier in finance with cutting-edge insights."

## Sub-Chapter 1: Fintech Innovation

Fintech technologies are transforming the financial industry by providing unprecedented opportunities for individuals and organizations to access financial services, streamline operations, and drive innovation. This sub-chapter delves into the use of disruptive technologies in finance, the investigation of opportunities in blockchain, artificial intelligence (AI), and machine learning, and the transformation of traditional financial services through fintech solutions.

- **Using disruptive technologies in finance**

disruptive technologies such as blockchain, artificial intelligence, machine learning, and big data analytics are altering the financial landscape by upending conventional business models, increasing efficiency, and fostering innovation. Both traditional financial institutions and fintech firms use these technologies to stay competitive and meet evolving client needs. Distributed ledger technology, for example, enables secure, open, and decentralized transactions using blockchain technology. It has the potential to revolutionize payment systems, supply chain financing, identity verification, and asset tokenization. Similarly, AI and machine learning algorithms offer robo-advisory services, fraud detection, credit rating, and personalized financial suggestions.

- **Exploring opportunities in machine learning, AI, and blockchain**

Blockchain, artificial intelligence, and machine learning opportunities are being explored, creating new avenues for innovation and disruption in the financial services industry. Smart contracts, digital asset exchanges, tokenized securities offerings, and decentralized finance (DeFi) platforms are all being made possible by blockchain technology.

Numerous financial applications, such as risk management, portfolio optimization, algorithmic trading, customer service automation, and regulatory compliance, are utilizing AI and machine learning algorithms. Financial institutions can now make data-driven choices, acquire greater insights, and improve consumer experiences thanks to these technologies.

- **Transforming traditional financial services with technology solutions**

Fintech solutions are altering traditional financial services by providing innovative products and services that address the changing demands of consumers and businesses. From mobile payments and peer-to-peer lending to robo-advisory platforms and digital banking solutions, fintech firms are disrupting incumbents and driving industry-wide change.

Traditional financial institutions are increasingly collaborating with or acquiring fintech companies to capitalize on their technological strengths and expedite digital transformation efforts. Traditional banks, insurance businesses, and asset managers can boost customer engagement, cut costs, and increase efficiency by incorporating fintech solutions into their portfolios.

Embracing the future of finance necessitates a proactive strategy to utilize fintech advances and disruptive technology. Individuals and businesses can position themselves at the forefront of the next frontier in finance by adopting blockchain, AI, and machine learning, exploring new opportunities, and transforming traditional financial services with fintech solutions.

## Sub-chapter 2: Decentralized Finance

Decentralized Finance (DeFi) is a game-changing paradigm change in the financial industry, providing a borderless, permissionless, and trustless alternative to traditional financial institutions. This subchapter digs into the foundations of decentralized finance, examines DeFi applications such as decentralized exchanges and lending platforms, and evaluates the dangers and prospects of DeFi investing.

- **Understanding the Principles of Decentralized Finance**

Decentralized finance, or DeFi, is a system of financial apps and protocols built on blockchain technology that aims to democratize access to financial services, eliminate middlemen, and advance financial inclusion.Transparency, interoperability, and censorship resistance are the principles on which DeFi operates.

Unlike traditional finance, which relies on centralized intermediaries such as exchanges, clearinghouses, and banks, DeFi protocols use decentralized networks and smart contracts to facilitate value transfer, asset issuance, and peer-to-peer transactions. As a result, consumers can acquire financial services directly and without the intervention of trustworthy third parties.

- **Exploring DeFi applications, such as lending platforms and decentralized exchanges**

While DeFi encompasses a wide range of services and applications, lending platforms and decentralized exchanges (DEXs) are two of the best-known examples. Decentralized exchanges allow users to transact digital assets directly with one another, eliminating the need for centralized middlemen to manage money or transactions.

DeFi lending systems, which use smart contracts, allow users to borrow and lend digital assets at interest rates determined by supply and demand dynamics. By providing liquidity to lending pools, users can earn interest or use their assets as collateral to borrow money. These platforms allow people and businesses to gain unrestricted access to liquidity and generate yield.

- **Assessing the opportunities and risks of investing in DeFi**

DeFi has enormous potential for financial inclusion and innovation, but it also has some inherent risks that investors must be aware of. Smart contract vulnerabilities, liquidity problems, market volatility, regulatory uncertainty, and the danger of financial loss due to hacking or protocol exploitation are among the risks connected with DeFi.

Despite these risks, investing in DeFi provides an excellent opportunity for investors to reap attractive benefits, participate in governance procedures, and gain exposure to cutting-edge financial products and services. Investors can minimize risk and maximize DeFi's potential by conducting thorough due diligence, diversifying their holdings, and staying current on industry trends.

Decentralized finance, or DeFi, is a disruptive force in the financial industry that offers a decentralized alternative to traditional financial institutions. People and businesses can participate in this revolutionary movement and open up new avenues for financial innovation and inclusivity by understanding the fundamentals of DeFi, researching applications such as decentralized marketplaces and lending systems, and weighing the potential benefits and drawbacks of DeFi investments.

# Sub-Chapter 3: Sustainable Finance

Sustainable finance, often known as responsible or ethical investing, is a developing trend in the financial industry that aims to include environmental, social, and governance (ESG) factors in investment decisions. This subchapter looks at how to include environmental and social factors in investment decisions, as well as how to promote sustainable enterprises and green initiatives and invest in renewable energy and climate resilience projects.

- **Integrating social and environmental factors in investment decisions**

Integrating environmental, social, and governance (ESG) considerations into investment research and decision-making procedures is known as sustainable finance. In addition to financial performance, investors assess a company's social responsibility, environmental effects, and corporate governance policies.

A company's water use, waste management procedures, energy efficiency, and carbon footprint are a few examples of environmental factors. Social factors might include community involvement, diversity, human rights, and labor norms. The focus of governance considerations is on things like executive salary, board independence, and openness.

- **Supporting environmentally conscious businesses and projects**

Sustainable finance provides support to enterprises that demonstrate a commitment to sustainability, social responsibility, and ethical business practices. Investors may be interested in companies that prioritize environmental sustainability, social justice, and long-term profit creation for all stakeholders.

Investors can support sustainable firms in several ways, including direct investment, impact investing, and shareholder involvement. Impact investors lend money to companies, projects, or funds that benefit society and the environment while also making a profit. Shareholder participation in corporate governance processes is essential to fostering transparent and moral business practices.

- **Financing climate resilience and renewable energy initiatives**

One of the key goals of sustainable finance is to invest in climate resilience and renewable energy projects that address environmental problems like resource depletion and climate change. Initiatives that use geothermal, hydroelectric, wind, and solar energy to generate power are examples of renewable energy investments.

Investors can provide financing for renewable energy projects using a range of vehicles, including renewable energy investment trusts, green bonds, and infrastructure funds. In addition to providing investors with attractive returns and diversity, these investments also contribute to the reduction of greenhouse gas emissions.

Sustainable finance encourages investments in climate resilience initiatives that help communities and businesses better prepare for the effects of climate change, such as rising sea levels, harsh weather, and water scarcity. This is in addition to renewable energy.

Sustainable finance emphasizes the incorporation of governance, social, and environmental factors into investment decisions, marking a paradigm shift in the financial sector. Investments in renewable energy and climate resilience projects, as well as sustainable business and green initiatives, can help investors achieve both financial gains and beneficial social and environmental results for coming generations.

# Subchapter 4: The Globalization of Finance

The globalization of finance has altered the financial landscape, ushering in a period of unprecedented interconnection and opportunity. This sub-chapter delves into the challenges of managing the changing global financial landscape, responding to regulatory changes and geopolitical developments, and capitalizing on possibilities in emerging markets and international commerce.

- **Managing the Changing Global Financial Landscape**

Technological discoveries, economic trends, and geopolitical challenges all have an impact on the ever-changing global financial landscape. To effectively identify opportunities and mitigate risks, financial institutions, investors, and legislators must navigate this dynamic environment.

Technological innovation, such as blockchain and artificial intelligence, is driving global financial growth. These technologies are reshaping financial services and market infrastructure. Economic shifts, such as changes in consumer behavior and market expansion, are reshaping global trade and investment patterns. Geopolitical variables such as trade tensions and regulatory reforms influence regulatory frameworks and market sentiment.

- **Adapting to regulatory and geopolitical shifts**

Regulatory changes and geopolitical movements have a significant impact on global finance, affecting market stability, investor confidence, and cross-border transactions. Financial institutions must remain watchful and modify their strategy to meet changing rules and overcome geopolitical concerns. Regulatory changes, such as modifications to banking legislation, capital requirements, and data protection standards, can have an impact on financial institutions' compliance costs and operating efficiencies. Geopolitical upheavals, such as trade wars, sanctions, and political unrest, can all impact global supply networks, cash flows, and investor mood.

- **Taking advantage of opportunities in global trade and emerging markets**

Because of developing economies and international trade, there is plenty of room for growth and diversification in global finance. Rapid urbanization, demographic transitions, and increased technological usage in emerging economies are driving demand for consumer goods, financial services, and infrastructure investment.

Investing in high-growth industries such as technology, healthcare, and renewable energy, as well as diversifying their portfolios across locations, allows investors to profit from developing market opportunities. Firms can use international sourcing and distribution networks to optimize supply chains, reach new markets, and increase their market presence through global trade.

Financial institutions, investors, and enterprises now have more opportunities because of the globalization of finance, but there are also difficulties in negotiating regulatory complexity, geopolitical unpredictability, and market volatility. Stakeholders may take advantage of the opportunities presented by global finance and support sustainable economic growth and prosperity by remaining knowledgeable, adaptable, and proactive.

## Subchapter 5: Financial Wellness

Financial wellness is critical for anyone seeking long-term financial security, peace of mind, and overall well-being. This sub-chapter focuses on supporting financial literacy and wellness efforts, empowering people to make educated financial decisions, and fostering resilient financial futures through education and empowerment.

- **Promoting wellness and financial literacy initiatives**

Financial literacy is the foundation of financial wellness, as it provides people with the knowledge and skills they need to manage their money sensibly, understand core financial concepts, and make sound financial decisions. Encourage financial literacy and wellness activities by providing programs, resources, and educational materials to help people improve their financial literacy.

Financial literacy initiatives may take the form of seminars, workshops, online classes, or instructional materials on topics such as insurance, investing, debt management, retirement planning, and budgeting. Employers, educational institutions, community organizations, and financial institutions must all work together to promote financial literacy and provide individuals with the tools they need to manage their finances.

- **Empowering individuals to make informed financial decisions**

Individuals must be empowered to make educated financial decisions by giving them the knowledge, confidence, and tools they need to properly navigate difficult financial choices. Financial empowerment entails developing a financial independence, self-reliance, and resilience mindset when it comes to personal finance management.

Financial empowerment efforts may involve individualized financial coaching, one-on-one counseling, and access to online tools and information that assist individuals in setting financial objectives, developing action plans, and tracking success over time. Individuals who are empowered to take charge of their financial destinies can overcome financial problems, achieve their goals, and develop a sense of financial stability and well-being.

- **Creating a secure financial future through empowerment and education**

To create financially resilient futures for individuals, we must provide them with the information, behaviors, and resources they need to deal with life's ups and downs. It demands a complete financial wellness strategy that considers mental, behavioral, and emotional health, as well as financial knowledge. Financial wellness programs may incorporate psychology, behavioral economics, and coaching to help people overcome barriers to financial success such as emotional decision-making, impulsivity, and procrastination. People can achieve long-term financial well-being and recover stronger by developing resilience, adaptability, and optimism when dealing with financial setbacks.

To prosper in the complicated and unpredictable financial world of today, people must be financially well. We can create a society where everyone has the information, skills, and confidence to reach their financial goals and live life to the fullest by supporting financial literacy and wellness initiatives, enabling people to make wise financial decisions, and constructing resilient financial futures through empowerment and education.

# CONCLUSION

In this comprehensive investigation of advanced finance, we addressed a wide range of topics, including risk management approaches, sustainable finance, welcoming the future of finance, and fostering financial well-being. We've learned valuable lessons and useful advice along the way, allowing people to confidently and efficiently navigate the complexities of the financial world.

The book's major takeaway is that, in today's rapidly changing financial landscape, education is your most precious asset. Understanding sophisticated financial concepts such as risk management, quantitative analysis, and financial engineering allows people to make informed decisions, decrease risks, and capitalize on development prospects.

We've also emphasized the importance of implementing cutting-edge technologies such as blockchain and artificial intelligence, as well as sustainable investing and decentralized financing. These advances provide the financial sector with new chances for growth, creativity, and value creation.

Furthermore, we have emphasized the importance of supporting financial health and literacy initiatives so that people may take control of their financial future. People may build a solid foundation for the future and successfully handle financial crises by creating a mindset of continuous learning, adaptation, and resilience.

Remember that learning is a lifetime activity as you go out on your incredible financial adventure, equipped with information and confidence. In the constantly changing world of finance, maintain your curiosity, knowledge, and adaptability. Accept change, grab chances, and work toward success and financial well-being.

You may steer clear of financial difficulties and build a better future for yourself and your loved ones by putting the ideas and tactics in this book into practice. With bravery, then, set out on your financial adventure and discover the countless opportunities that lie ahead in the world of finance.

www.ingramcontent.com/pod-product-compliance
Lightning Source LLC
Chambersburg PA
CBHW050104230526
45470CB00004B/1675